702695

375.

THE GRAMMAR SCHOOL TRADITION
IN A COMPREHENSIVE WORLD

The Grammar School Tradition in a Comprehensive World

J. N. HEWITSON

London
ROUTLEDGE & KEGAN PAUL

First published in 1969
by Routledge and Kegan Paul Ltd
Broadway House, 68–74 Carter Lane
London, E.C.4
Printed in Great Britain by
Western Printing Services Ltd, Bristol
© J. N. Hewitson 1969
SBN 7100 6392 x

Contents

Acknowledgements

I am grateful to the Master and Fellows of Downing College, Cambridge, and to my employers, the City of Norwich Education Committee, whose combined generosity made it possible for me to spend a term as a Schoolmaster Fellow Commoner at Cambridge, which alone made it possible for me to write this book.

To
Jean and Elizabeth

I

Introduction

'That branch of lying which consists of very nearly deceiving your friends without quite deceiving your enemies', is Cornford's immortal definition of the art of propaganda; and as all sections of the community have blazed away at each other during the recent controversies on Comprehensive Reorganization of Secondary Schools—theorists, politicians, administrators, teachers and parents, generating far more heat than light with their conflicting claims—I have often been reminded of it. As Headmaster of a large grammar school directly involved, and therefore near to the warring heart of the controversy, I have probably been as guilty as anyone; and I think it is high time that we settled down to a period of quieter reflection, and worked out in sober terms what it is all likely to mean.

Much of what I have to say is bound to have some oblique reference to the sizeable number of children of all ages attending schools in the private sector, although they are not my direct concern. The children in full-time attendance at state or local authority schools in the public sector most certainly are— and there are some seven million of these, almost three million of whom are attending various types of maintained secondary schools in England and Wales. It is these schools, and these children who will be most directly and immediately affected by the change-over to comprehensive schools which is proceeding apace all over the country. It is these changes as they are likely to affect these children which we so desperately need to get into proper perspective.

That means, of course, providing a perspective into which

I

the changes can be put, and to do this we need to look at the way the state system of schools has evolved over the years; since what happened, and more importantly, what did not happen in 1870, 1902, and 1944, helps to explain the strengths and weaknesses of the present system of schools which we are now busy replacing. It may be, too, that the past is much more immediately relevant to the future than many people are prepared to admit. It would be wrong, of course, to allow the past to dominate the future, but it is equally foolhardy to disregard entirely the lessons that it has to teach. For instance, there is the immense amount of toil and effort needed to build up the state schools to the standard which they have so far reached, a standard which may or may not satisfy us, but would astound the early pioneers if they could come back to see it. There is no magic wand which can of itself bring about a marked and immediate improvement in future standards without even more toil and greater efforts, however much we try to persuade ourselves to the contrary. Then again, it is as well to note the perverse way in which the best of ideas can go wrong in practice, and produce results diametrically opposite to what was intended. The notorious Eleven Plus, for example, started life as the brain child of the most progressive educationists of the time, but their bright new device for unlocking the doors of privilege for the poor boy and girl was twisted into something else quite different. There are bad things in the field of education, but they are not half so pernicious as good ideas (particularly yesterday's good ideas) carelessly or thoughtlessly applied. Is this, then, an argument against all change? By no means, since the entire pattern of development of state schooling in this country has been a story of change, and it would be quite wrong to assume, as many people do, that any type of state school has ever been left unchanged for long. As the economic and social development of the country has placed new demands upon them, schools changed as they are changing now—but, and it is a melancholy thought, however fast they changed they could never quite catch up with current ideas, nor were they ever given the resources which would have allowed them to do so.

All this should put us on our guard against expecting too much, too easily, too cheaply, too quickly from our present plans for reorganization. I spend a good deal of time explaining how one local authority painfully hammered out its own administrative machine for Comprehensive Reorganization. I do not suggest for a moment that the methods it adopted, the lines of argument it followed, and the solutions it came up with are relevant to all authorities in all circumstances. They are not. Indeed, some of the solutions it so indignantly rejected may with other authorities in other circumstances be far more practical than the scheme it chose. But I am suggesting that some such painful stage has got to be gone through before an idea can be turned into a practical administrative proposition; and whatever administrative pattern an authority finally adopts, this is only the first step. There must then be a detailed and far-reaching reorganization of the internal arrangements of every school, and I indicate in some detail the general lines this internal reorganization must follow. But there are so many possible variants in both administrative pattern and internal reorganization, that the facile notion that every area in this country will soon find itself with identical comprehensive schools, each one working along well-tried and identical lines to provide a commodity clearly recognizable as 'comprehensive education', quite different and markedly superior to anything which has gone before, is very wide of the mark. The result is much more likely to be—in fact, can not help but be—a patchwork quilt of bewildering variety, varying greatly from area to area, and with great, though we hope diminishing, inequalities within each area. The brand-new, purpose-built comprehensive school, fully equipped for its exciting task, will for years to come be a comparative rarity. For the next twenty years or so, the vast majority of children will be taught in buildings designed for quite different purposes, and the existing bricks and mortar will powerfully influence and limit the kind of education which can be given. It could not be otherwise, unless the country was prepared to direct a mammoth amount of its building resources to this one social service, and it is not.

It is necessary to say all this to counteract the unrealistic dreams of theorists and the undue optimism of local politicians, both of which can cause bitter disillusionment when the promised new heaven does not immediately appear. But I would not

3

defer to either of them in my profound belief that such a heaven does exist, and we ought to be taking steps towards it. In my last three chapters I indicate what some of these steps should be. Perhaps those steps will be of more use if we take care to see that in taking one step forward we don't slip two backward. By that, I mean that the better schools of the future must be developed from the best schools of today. In recent years there has been a steady improvement of standards in every type of secondary school, and as a practising teacher myself I am proud of what my fellow teachers have achieved in widely varied fields. Particularly is this so in the case of the much maligned grammar schools. I would not wish to deceive either my friends or my enemies about my feelings towards them. Unless the best of the Grammar School Tradition is somehow carried over into the new regime, then we will have slipped more steps backward than I care to think. But can they change to suit the new requirements? I do not see them myself as static, immovable, unalterable, isolated institutions. I notice that they have changed many times already through the years as society has required them to change, and I do not think they need falter at yet one more step in their historic development. The wise authority will see that they do not; the foolish authority will suffer for its sins. Yes I believe they can change, and yet remain essentially the same, and have taken time off to write this screed in hopes that the reader too may understand how this paradox can be possible. The task as I see it now is to strain every nerve to see that the essence of the grammar school lives on into the new scheme of things, and I return to the fray to see that it does, my head as well as that of the great institution I revere—'bloody but unbowed'.

2

The Perspective

The State system of Education in this country is less than one
hundred years old. It really dates from W. E. Forster's
Education Act of 1870, which insisted for the first time that all
children in this country ought to have some education, however
disjointed and elementary it might be; and that it was the duty
of the State to see that it was provided, if possible by somebody
else—by parents, by religious charities, by churches and
chapels, by philanthropic employers—but in the last resort
by the State. This was the extremely modest, almost timid
foundation on which has been built the system of State schools
as we know them today. How timid and modest this foundation
was will be clearer when we look at the provisions of the Act
in greater detail. Whilst it clearly stated that all children
ought to have some education, it did not say in so many words
that they *must*, and fell over backwards to disguise the element
of compulsion which had to be present in the Act to prevent
it being a complete dead letter. Yet it aroused the most bitter
and virulent opposition, and the violent political storms which
raged around it make our present controversy over comprehensive schools seem a polite little 'local disturbance' in
comparison. Far from being timid, it was in the context of
its own time an extremely courageous first step; and if it
seems to us a modest compromise, we have to realize that it had
to be fought for tooth and nail with consummate political
skill; and there were many occasions when it looked as though
it would never reach the statute book at all. To understand why

5

this should be, we need to have some idea, however sketchy, of what had gone before.

A great deal had gone before, and as good a place as any to start may be in pre-Reformation England. I think we would have been agreeably surprised at the standard of general education of our ancestors in those distant days. It seems to have been adequate for their purposes, and admirably suited to the political and social conditions of the times. There was, of course, no question of the State taking a leading part in it, since the nation state was only starting to be born itself. Transport difficulties ensured that it was a local matter, yet it was curiously international at the same time, since two of the principal educational forces (Chivalry and the Catholic Church) were international organizations. If I may hopelessly over-simplify to make what I believe is still a valid point, I would say that they had a tripartite system which powerfully affected educational development in this country for centuries, and still keeps cropping up in unexpected places today.

Firstly there was the education of Chivalry. If you were sufficiently well born you became a page, or an apprentice gentleman, and were given an intensive, mainly outdoor, training to fit you for your station in life. The page was, according to theory, drilled in the 'seven free arts'—riding, swimming, boxing hawking, archery, chess, and verse-making. The object was to produce soldiers, leaders, and feudal administrators. The great emphasis was on character training and manliness, and the principal subjects of the curriculum, taught by the most modern activity methods, were 'trouthe and honour, fredom and curtesie'. It was a laudable ambition, and at its best a fine tradition. Is it too fanciful to jump to 'Tom Brown's Schooldays' in 1857? Squire Brown, you will remember, after he had packed Tom off to Rugby, said, 'If only he'll turn out to be a brave, helpful, truth-telling Englishman, and a gentleman, and a Christian, that's all I want.'

Secondly, there was the education of the Church. It is difficult to appreciate fully the immense wealth and influence of the great, supranational monastic orders. As this developed they became the principal educative force. It was essential for the monks and clergy to have a minimum of book learning if they were to take part in the religious ceremonies and observances of their calling. It was even more important for them to have some secular instruction if they were to manage properly the great wealth which came into their possession, and the Church was astute enough to see that the secular 'know-how' and business expertise generated in the monastic schools was indispensable to the great feudal nobles, and properly used could give the Church great influence. Education was the Church's secret weapon; the pen was mightier than the sword. Even when schools began to be established by wealthy merchants and philanthropists outside the monasteries—and even when the monasteries themselves had disappeared—the Church held on to its influence in this sphere, and it was not until the reign of Queen Victoria that it finally became legal to teach in an English School without first securing a Bishop's licence to do so.

Whilst the education of Chivalry was almost exclusively a class affair, the education offered by the Church in these early days was much more democratic, and it was prepared to take its pupils from all sections of society. There were many cases of poor scholars rising to positions of the greatest eminence inside and outside the Church. The son of a Suffolk peasant became Bishop of Lincoln and a famous statesman in the reign of Henry III. Edmund Rich, a poor boy from Abingdon became Archbishop of Canterbury, whilst the son of a servant at the Abbey of St. Albans became Pope Adrian IV. The monastic schools were supposed in theory to base their work on the 'seven liberal arts'—grammar, logic, rhetoric, music, geometry, astronomy, and arithmetic. Their object was to produce statesmen, clergy, clerks, lawyers, civil servants, and accountants. Though the direct theological influence of the Church and its teachings has now largely disappeared from our modern schools, the traditional connection is still very much alive, as can be seen by the tacit expectation of society that every school shall continue to exert a strong moral influence on its pupils.

Thirdly, there was the education of the vast majority of the ordinary people of those days. It is tempting to jump to the conclusion that schooling for them was non-existent, but this would not be strictly true. Evidence exists that the luckier and the brighter could pick up a smattering, and in the smaller towns and villages there was usually a reading or song school, like the 'little scole' Chaucer tells about in the 'Prioress's Tale', in which there were 'children an heep',

> That lerned in that scole yeare by yeare,
> Swich maner doctrine as men used there,
> This is to seyn, to singen and to rede,
> As smale children doon in hir childhede.

We must not forget, either, the well-developed system of apprenticeship which flourished so strongly under the medieval merchant guilds, and provided technical, vocational, and social training of a high order. Indeed, Professor Gertrude Williams, writing on 'The Recruitment to Skilled Trades' in 1957, was rather ruefully able to say, 'The present system of recruiting and training young workers for skilled industry is—in all essential points—exactly the same as the method introduced more than 800 years ago for an entirely different economy.' But none of this should blind us to the fact that the education of the people in pre-Reformation times was neglected. Dangerous thinkers like Wycliffe, for instance, maintained that it was high time that the nobles and the embryo state did intervene, and suggested that the wealth of the religious houses should be diverted to provide better education for the common people. He also, incidentally, suggested that girls as well as boys should be catered for, but he was a voice crying in the wilderness, and the education of the mass of the people continued to be grossly neglected for another four centuries.

The Reformation itself did nothing for the education of the common people, and not a great deal for the education of any other class either. The Renaissance which accompanied it was also a mixed blessing. Sir Cyril Norwood in his book *The English Tradition of Education*, says:

The Renaissance and the Reformation were both disintegrating influences. The Renaissance by itself might have been an inspiration, for it brought in a more living curriculum and more valuable subjects of study. But it also brought with it much individualism, and questioned the principles of the old loyalties to Church and State. It was the Reformation which in this country dealt the hardest blow to education. It broke up the unity of the nation. The Catholics were outlawed and persecuted, and the Protestants broke into sects. Many schools were plundered and destroyed, and a spirit of self-seeking, of private profit to be made at the expense of the public benefit was let loose. By the end of the reign of Elizabeth, many of the schools were refounded, but in a different spirit, with smaller resources and less opportunity. They were for one class—the sons of the members of the Established Church. There was no access for the sons of Catholics and Nonconformists. The old ideals were lost sight of, and the seventeenth and eighteenth centuries are a dark period in the history of English education. A Milton or a Locke might theorize about education, but the inside of the schools of the nation was given over to a narrow curriculum of much Latin and a little Greek, handled with increasing stupidity by clerical pedagogues of low status. Many seem to have had no higher ideals than to teach grammar and repetition with the aid of the birch. Their pay was a pittance, their classes impossibly large, and they left their boys to shape their own characters. Here and there, *rari nantes in gurgite vasto*, were nobler spirits, but the nation as a whole was surrendered to a hard and fast system of privilege, the government of a political oligarchy, and to a system of thought in which spiritual values had been largely forgotten.

It was this disintegration, and the bitter passions which it had aroused, which was at the heart of the violent opposition which met Forster's Act of 1870 when he presented it to the House.

These passions had been kept alight, and the disintegration of the schools accelerated by the extraordinary economic, social, and political changes which swept across an unsuspecting England during the second half of the eighteenth century and the early years of the nineteenth. The pace at which these changes happened, and their revolutionary nature, had no equal in our previous history. Revolutionary methods of farming required large enclosed farms, and displaced the old system of open-field farming that for centuries had been carried on by yeomen, or small farmers, and their labourers. Mechanical inventions superseded the hard work of home industries, and the industrial revolution created factories and mills. Where coal and iron were found together, villages exploded into great towns. Communications were improved as a network of canals was dug to join the manufacturing regions to each other, pack-horse tracks became broad metalled roads, and the first railway was opened (1825). There was a rapid over-all increase of the population. Whilst great fortunes were made in industry, and a well-to-do middle class of manufacturers and business men was created, the majority of the working population found themselves herded together in circumstances of incredible filth and squalor. The French wars, first against the Republic and afterwards Napoleon, strained the resources of the country to the utmost, and led to war-weariness, unemployment, and discontent. The existing grammar schools (descendants of the old monastic schools) were less and less useful to the masters, since their narrow, exclusively classical curriculum, had no relevance to the new sciences and technologies; whilst the men were being brutalized, and educational provision for them was either inadequate or non-existent.

As the inevitably bitter resentment grew, stern repression of the workers grew less and less effective. The 'dangerous' ideas of the French Revolution appealed more and more, and some people felt political action was the only way out. Not the least of the demands of the politicians of the French Revolution was for 'Education universal, compulsory, gratuitous, and secular'; there could hardly be more comprehensive demands. Doctrinaire left-wing politicians in this country set out to achieve just this by direct political action, and are still active trying to achieve it today. In fact, part of the storm which broke over Forster's head was generated by the ill-temper and petulance of these people, who regarded themselves as being the most advanced section of political thought in the country, and were appalled to find that as late as 1870 they still had not got anywhere near what they had been demanding.

Others, sceptical of achieving much by political action, or genuinely convinced that this was not a political matter at all, felt impelled to take direct social action. Philanthropic employers like Robert Owen experimented in providing better conditions and educational training in model factories. It was better for business to have contented and intelligent work people, apart from the little matter of helping your fellow men. They were less likely to burn down your mill, or destroy your machinery, so it was better for civil peace. It was, too, an interesting piece of social engineering. An intellectual and moral revolution was also taking place, and the ideas of Locke, Rousseau, and Bentham were avidly discussed. Particularly powerful was the psychological notion of the 'tabula rasa'.

This was the idea that when a man was born his mind was a
blank sheet, on which was painted a picture by the environment
in which he found himself and the experiences of his subsequent
life. All you had to do was to control the environment and the
experiences and you could control the kind of man into which
the child grew. Do that with enough men and women and you
had radically altered society. It was true that Locke, who had
put forward this notion, had said something else as well.
He had pointed out that 'nature' had to be considered as well
as 'nurture', but this was conveniently forgotten. Radical
thinkers who passionately believed that they had found in
universal education the key to the perfectibility of mankind
formed what came to be known as 'the Educationally mad party'
—but mad or sane, misguided or sensible, they provided a great
deal of steam for the growing agitation for education for the
masses for its own sake, not just as an antidote to crime, a
political drug, or a business proposition. These radical thinkers
were not confined to the wealthier classes, and quite apart from
the efforts of philanthropic employers, the workers themselves
showed surprising energy in helping themselves whenever half
a chance appeared. A London Mechanics Institute opened in a
disused chapel in 1824, and it had 1,887 students within twelve
months. Similar Mechanics Institutes were opened at Glasgow,
Liverpool, Manchester, Leeds—to mention but a few. Some of
these Institutes started up their own day schools. Even the
State itself timidly began to consider that it might do something
to help. At the instigation of two mill owners—Sir Robert
Peel and Robert Owen—Parliament passed in 1802 'An Act
for the preservation of the health and morals of apprentices
and others employed in cotton and other mills and cotton and
other factories'. The working day of these young people was not
to exceed twelve hours, excluding meals, and during the first
four years of their seven-year apprenticeship, time had to be
found during the working day for some elementary instruction
in reading, writing, arithmetic, and scripture. The Act aroused
howls of protest from industry, and was little better than a
dead letter since there was no machinery to enforce it. But it
was a start, and as we shall see led to bigger things.

However, the greatest contribution at this time to providing
schools for the majority of the people was made by the churches

and chapels: the old dissenting sects, the new Methodists, and the established church itself, if they were hopelessly disunited on doctrinal and theological matters, were united by a strong evangelical feeling urging them to better the brutish conditions of the poor. A Sunday School started at Gloucester in 1780 was copied in many other parts. In the thirties of the nineteenth century it was estimated that a million pupils, adults as well as children, attended school on Sundays. They were taught to read the Bible, but other books, and the teaching of writing and arithmetic began to creep in. Some Sunday Schools were so successful that they were opened on week-day evenings too, and it was not long till modest day schools began to be founded in go-ahead parishes. Writing in 1847, Kay-Shuttleworth said that the Sunday School had 'laid the foundations of public education for the poor deeply in the religious organizations of the country. The type of this school has to a great extent predetermined the constitution of the daily school, and provided the fabric which by a natural transition may be employed in the establishment of an efficient system of elementary instruction.'

Local efforts to found such daily schools were co-ordinated by national societies. The Dissenters formed the 'Institution for Promoting the British System for the Education of the Labouring and Manufacturing Classes of Society of Every Religious Persuasion', mercifully changing the title to the British and Foreign Schools Society in 1814. The Established Church set up 'The National Society for the Education of the Poor in the Principles of the Established Church throughout England and Wales', which came to be known as the National Society. Between them, occasionally in harmony, but more often in jealous competition, these two societies set themselves the heroic task of attempting to provide elementary education throughout the entire country, at a time when the burden of doing so was increasing very rapidly. They borrowed ideas which would have been more appropriate to industry to help them in their task. If factories flourished by division of labour, so could schools. They welcomed the Monitorial System, whereby the master taught a small group of brighter pupils, and then sent them off to teach their fellows. By this means, it was estimated, one trained teacher could handle a class of up to 1,000 children. But of course, in practice, it did not quite work out like that. They made every effort to raise money to found more and more schools. Court fines were shared in one parish, street lamps farmed out in another. In one case the nitrous earth was collected from the boys' lavatories and sold to gun-powder makers. But the task was really beyond them.

Could the State not help? In 1807, Samuel Whitbread introduced a Bill into Parliament which, if it had been accepted, would have set up a national system of rate-aided Elementary Education, but it was thrown out by the House of Lords, largely on the advice of the Archbishop of Canterbury, who strongly objected to the control of education being anywhere else than in the hands of the bishop of a diocese. A similar Bill presented in 1820 by Lord Brougham was also defeated, this time because the Dissenters distrusted State interference, which they felt would work against them and in favour of the Established Church. In 1833, Roebuck brought forward another Bill, but it met the same fate. Frontal assault was clearly impossible, so subterfuge and stealth were tried. A small item was tacked on to the budget of 1833, providing £20,000 which could be used to help private subscribers of any denomination who were thinking of setting up a school. Ironically, the principal opponent in a half empty House was William Cobbett. He felt that educating the people merely increased crime, and that increasing the number of teachers would create a new race of idle lay-abouts.

But the State had intervened in the field of Elementary Education, and as might have been expected, the size of the grant grew from year to year. A special committee of the Privy Council was set up to control the distribution of the grant, and a few inspectors were appointed to tour the country to see that the grant was properly used. In a fit of absence of mind, a Department of Education had just happened. In 1856 it was given its official representative in the House of Commons— whose title was 'The Vice President of the Committee of the Privy Council on Education'. In 1858 the Newcastle Commission was set up to find out exactly what was going on. It was asked to report on 'the state of popular education in England, and as to the measures required for an extension of sound and cheap elementary instruction'. It found that in spite of the money being spent by the two Societies and the State, the great majority of children in the country were not learning the three Rs. The situation varied markedly from school to school and area to area, and in some places they were not only learning their three Rs but a great deal more besides. Moreover the statistics on which the Commission were compelled to rely were very far from being accurate. But the four volumes of the laboriously constructed report made clear—what should have been obvious already—that the hotch-potch arrangements were inadequate to cope with a problem of this size. The Commission made a series of recommendations which Parliament blandly ignored.

But Robert Lowe, the Vice President of the Committee of the Privy Council on Education, seized on one of the least fortunate of the Commission's recommendations, and put it into effect by administrative action immediately. The grant to each School was now to be directly dependent on an examination of its pupils carried out by H.M. Inspector. Failure to reach the required standard in the three Rs, for whatever reason, meant no grant. This was the infamous 'payment by results'. As Lowe said of his Revised Code, 'If the new system will not be cheap, it will be efficient, and if it will not be efficient, it will be cheap.'

There was, of course, a third alternative. Lowe's Revised Code might be both cheap and inefficient; and it was. The State Grant, which had risen from the original £20,000 of 1833 to £930,000 in 1859, had been cut back to £656,000 in 1865. But this was an under-capitalized service to start with, and it was a growing service, not a contracting one. Although the grant was reduced the demand for help increased, and something like 1,500 more schools were opened during Lowe's regime. But the quality of the teaching sadly deteriorated. The curriculum was cut to the bare bone to concentrate on the all important three Rs. Matthew Arnold, one of H.M. Inspectors, and in a good position to judge said, 'The mode of teaching in the primary schools' (by which he meant the elementary schools) 'has fallen off in intelligence, spirit, and inventiveness. It could not well be otherwise.' There were other interesting side-effects. H.M. Inspectors, for instance, became terrifying bogey men throughout the elementary schools—an attitude to them which persisted for generations, and is not yet completely dead. Again, it was firmly not to say ruthlessly established that these schools must be run on the cheap whatever else happened, and this lesson bit deeply into the consciousness of these schools, and is still warping the spirit of their descendants today, even though attitudes and circumstances have changed completely. And finally, the Revised Code led to such a rumpus that Robert Lowe had to resign, and the new man, W. E. Forster, was given the chance to introduce his Education Act.

This was a masterly attempt at a common-sense compromise. It attempted to disarm criticism by taking the line that it was merely 'filling in the gaps' in the provision of schools. The voluntary schools which already existed—precious vested interests of all denominations—were to continue as before. They would continue to charge their pupils fees (if this was appropriate and possible), continue to raise money by private subscription, and the State Grant in aid would continue, but would be increased. In areas where the need was too great to be satisfied by the voluntary schools, a new body was to be set up. This was an elective School Board. It would be authorized to build and run the necessary additional schools, paying for them by charging the pupils fees (not exceeding 9d. per week), by a Government Grant, and by levying a local rate. It was the local rate which was new, and might arouse criticism, so Forster attempted to disarm it by declaring that a 3d. rate would rarely be exceeded, that better education would bring about a corresponding reduction in the prison and pauper rate, and that in any case the education rate was not a new one, but a charge on the existing poor rate fund. This insistence on the origin of Elementary Schools as an off-shoot of the Poor Law, taken with Lowe's insistence that they must be run on the cheap, powerfully affected the public attitude towards them, and when a later Government in 1944 declared that they were no longer elementary schools, but secondary modern schools, and worthy of the same esteem as the grammar schools, a sceptical public refused to believe it. An attempt was made to settle the religious squabbles, or at least to hammer out a compromise which all could accept, with good or bad grace. No religious teaching was to be imposed on a child in a Board School if his parents objected. To make it possible for the parent to withdraw his

15

child from any such teaching without the child suffering, such religious teaching had to be given at either the beginning or the end of a school session. Such religious teaching as was given in a Board School was to be non-doctrinal and non-sectarian. The Act stopped short of compelling parents to send their children to school. This would have savoured too much of interfering with the rights of the individual. But it gave the local School Boards the power to frame by-laws compelling the parents of children between certain ages to send them to school, unless they could provide some reasonable excuse. It was up to the local School Board to decide whether it wanted to use this power, and if it did, what it was prepared to accept as a reasonable excuse. At the centre of the web there was to be a State Department responsible for the efficient running of the elementary schools of the country—and all schools in receipt of a Government grant were to be open to inspection by H.M. Inspectors to ensure that they were efficient; but as can be seen, the emphasis was all on the decentralization of control to the School Boards, the Voluntary Managers, and the parents.

Forster's compromise established a pattern for the Schools of this country which can still be recognized today. It was a solid success, and within the next twenty years the average school attendance rose from one and a quarter million to four and a half million. But it failed to satisfy the principal contestants. Both church and chapel were upset that doctrinal teaching—their particular doctrine—was to be excluded from Board Schools. They felt too that the Board Schools would increase at such a rate that they would not be able to compete, and the denominational schools would become of less and less importance. They were right, of course, to be sceptical that the State could limit its activities to 'filling in the gaps'. More Radical spirits regarded Forster's Bill as a sell out, falling far short of their historic demand for 'Education, universal, compulsory, and secular'. Was it right to levy rates on them for state schools, and then use part of this rate to provide religious instruction however non-doctrinal? This particular argument is still unsettled today. Their other grouses have long since been taken care of: in 1880 Elementary Education was made compulsory for all, and in 1891 it was offered free of expense. But none of this was clear in 1870, and Forster's party lost

16

the next election. It was a small price to pay for such a seminal piece of social legislation, though I don't imagine Forster's colleagues saw it in this light. Faced by 'children an heep', Forster had arranged for them to have 'a little scole'. A wealthy merchant who had made his fortune in Bradford, he also in due course arranged for Manchester to have its Ship Canal. It was a remarkable treble! When he left office in 1874 he had added 4,982 schools to the 8,281 that existed when he took office. As he said, 'some education is now secured to all English children. Whether that some is enough to be of real value is now the question; but I do not think the work can stop.'

ADEQUATE EDUCATION FOR ALL

'The work', as Forster called it, did not stop. The School Boards and the various denominations and voluntary bodies continued to expand and increase the provision of Elementary Education in this country. But it is important to remember the limited aims. This was intended to be the minimum education considered necessary for the children of the labouring classes and the deserving poor, to enable them in due course to take their 'rightful' place in society as the labouring classes and deserving poor of the next generation. This was provision for parents unable to provide for their own children. If a parent could provide, then he sent his children to schools in the private sector; and it was in these schools only that was provided what was known in those days as Secondary Education.

It was quite different from what we understand by Secondary Education today, though the obvious social over-tones have not yet completely disappeared. For one thing, the elementary school in those days did not lead on to the secondary school, except in unusual circumstances. Elementary and Secondary were two parallel lines which were not expected to meet: each system (in so far as either was a system) complete, or incomplete, in itself, providing for, or failing to provide for different social classes. When a small group of Headmasters from the leading schools in the private, or secondary, sector came together in December 1869 to form the Headmasters' Conference to look after the interests of their secondary schools, there was a great gulf between them and the various existing associations of teachers who, in June 1870, formed themselves into the National Union of Elementary School Teachers (now the N.U.T.) to safeguard the interests of their elementary schools. They were poles apart, and though the gulf today is infinitely less than it was then, it has still not completely disappeared.

What was meant by Secondary Education in 1870, and where did one send one's child if one wanted it? The answer to both these questions is to be found in the reports of the Clarendon Commission (1864) and the Taunton Commission (1868), which surveyed the state of affairs in the existing endowed schools throughout the country. What a chaotic muddle it all was. For some hundreds of years before the middle of the eighteenth century, grammar schools had been set up by philanthropic patrons, intended in theory at least to act as feeder schools to the two ancient universities. Remember that it was customary to go up to University at the tender age of fifteen. In practice, however, the principal aim of the grammar school was to give some form of instruction in Latin, which down to the first half of the eighteenth century was still to a great extent the language of theology, law, science, and even diplomacy in Western Europe. But this severely limited curriculum became progressively out of touch with the real needs of the times. 'The most precious years', said a critic in the *Edinburgh Review* of 1830, 'are spent, not in filling the mind with solid knowledge; not in training it to habits of correct patient thought; but in a course of half-studious idleness, of which the only lasting trace is the recollection of mis-spent time.' Even if one wanted to bring the curriculum up to date, one was prevented from doing so by the terms of the endowment laid down by the original benefactor. When the Headmaster of Leeds Grammar School wanted to use part of his endowment to hire teachers of French or German and to set up a subsidiary department for commercial training, Lord Eldon ruled in the Court of Chancery (1805) that he could not do so. Lord Eldon borrowed Dr. Johnson's definition of a Grammar School as a 'school in which the learned languages are taught grammatically', and refused to budge. Moreover, the distribution of endowed Grammar Schools throughout the country was bizarre and irregular. It depended on the whims of benefactors centuries before, and took no account of falling population in some areas, and rising population in others. The Master of the Whitgift Hospital, Croydon, for instance, found no pupils in the school when he was appointed, and had none during the thirty-odd years he was Master. When the Commissioners visited the school at Thame, they found two masters and one boy, and when they went to Normanton they found the master reading a sporting paper whilst his eleven pupils looked after themselves. These were obviously extreme cases, but the general picture was black. 'Viewed as a whole', said the Commissioners, 'the conditions of school education above the primary has been called a chaos, and the condition of the endowed schools is certainly not the least chaotic portion.' When one glories in the Grammar School tradition stretching way back into the mists of time, one ought to be at least aware that the mists are hiding quite a number of skeletons in the most respectable of cupboards.

Of course, the picture was not completely black. Nine perfectly ordinary local grammar schools had built up their reputations and their fees, and had become non-local and residential, and famous as the nine great public schools. Sticklers for tradition, and hide-bound though they at times became, they had thrown up educational innovators like Arnold of Rugby, Thring of Uppingham, and Butler of Shrewsbury. Though classics remained the important part of their curriculum, there had been some broadening and diversification. Rugby built a physics laboratory in 1859 for instance, and Uppingham a gymnasium in the same year. Possibly more important still, the work of Arnold and others in developing the corporate life of their schools did much to improve the image of this kind of school in the eyes of the upper middle classes, who welcomed the social and moral training that they now offered. This, coming at the same time as the development of railways, led to the floating of stock-holding companies to establish boarding or day schools of a similar pattern, known as Proprietary Schools. The best known were boarding schools such as Cheltenham, Marlborough, Rossall, Radley, Wellington and Haileybury, and day schools such as King's College School, City of London School, and Liverpool College. These new schools were not tied down by restrictive statutes of long-dead founders and benefactors, and were able to respond more readily to the vocational demands of their parents. There were also many parents of the middle and lower middle classes who could not afford to send their sons to the Public Schools, or to the more successful grammar schools, or to the new proprietary schools, and to cater for them new private boarding schools or day schools were set up. They provided a strictly utilitarian course of two or three years' duration, ostensibly as a preparation for a business career. But the ironic thing was that these new private schools which sprang up had quite often very low standards indeed, and were often inferior in every way to the Board Schools; so that in many cases a parent bought secondary education which was markedly inferior to that given in an elementary school.

The Clarendon Commission on the nine great Public Schools is in many respects a hair-raising document, but the Commissioners felt that on the whole it would be most unwise to try to alter the dominant position of classics in their curriculum.

For the instruction of boys, especially when collected in a large school, (they said), it is material that there should be some one principal branch of study, invested with a recognized and, if possible, a traditional importance, to which the principal weight should be assigned, and the largest share of time and attention given. We believe that this is necessary in order to concentrate attention to stimulate industry, to supply to the whole school a common ground of literary interest, and a common path of promotion. The study of the classical languages and literature at present occupies this position in all the great English schools. It has, as we have already observed, the advantage of long possession, an advantage so great that we would certainly hesitate to advise the dethronement of it, even if we were prepared to recommend a successor.

They continued to call for a 'common ground' and a 'common path of promotion' for all—showing no concern for the widely varying abilities and interests of these boys who had been gathered together largely by the accidents of birth and the ability of their parents to pay the fees. The boy had to be fitted to the course, not the course to the boy. Though the Commissioners did call for some liberalization of the curriculum, and pressed for greater time and attention to be given to other subjects, particularly science and modern languages, they had already bolted the stable door before the horse had had a

chance to get into it. Classics was still king, they had no
intention of 'dethroning' it, and as they could not conceive
anything else that could replace it, they didn't attempt to
suggest one. Thus, to all intents and purposes, the real study of
science was practically excluded from the education of the
ruling classes in England for at least another generation—'a
plain defect and a great practical evil'.

The Taunton Commission on the remaining endowed schools
of the country was equally disturbing. Of the old endowed
schools in England and Wales—there were 782 of them—
only 209 of them were really giving a recognizable classical
education. 183 of them gave a semi-classical education, but
taught almost no Greek. 340 of them taught neither Latin
nor Greek, and seldom gave satisfactory instruction in Mathematics, French, or Science. In fact, the majority of these 340
schools gave an education which was certainly no better and
often inferior to that of an ordinary elementary school. Amongst
this rag bag of thoroughly disorganized and unsatisfactory
secondary schools, the Commissioners strove manfully to
unravel guide lines of some kind. They decided that the key
to this Chinese puzzle should be the length of time a parent
was prepared to keep his son at school. 'Education can at present
be classified as that which is to stop at about 14, that which is
to stop at about 16, and that which is to continue till 18 or
19; and for convenience we shall call these the third, the second,
and the first grade of education respectively.' First grade
schools, with a leaving age of 19 were to teach the classics
as a principal requirement, and to aim at continuing a close
connection with the universities. They were intended to
cater for the upper classes. Second grade schools with a leaving
age of 16 or 17 would make Latin an important subject, and in
addition teach two modern languages. They were to cater
particularly for the middle classes. Third grade schools with a
leaving age of 14 or 15 should still teach a modicum of Latin
and the beginnings of a foreign language, but apart from that
could conform to whatever the local requirements seemed to be.
They were intended 'for the whole of the lower portion of what
is commonly called the middle class'. It is important once again
to stress the avowed class consciousness of secondary education
at this time. There were to be four clearly recognized kinds of

school, with the Public Schools at the top of the pyramid. How else, reasoned the nineteenth-century mind, could you cater for the four superior grades of society, except by giving them a separate school for their separate needs? With this strong theme running right through the nineteenth century and beyond, it is not surprising to find in the second half of the twentieth century that the concept of a common secondary school for the boys and girls of all social classes stirs up bitter resentments. Secondary education for girls, by the way, was at this time practically non-existent. The Commissioners found only 13 endowed secondary schools for girls in the entire country. They recommended that something should be done, and gradually the campaign for educating girls got under way. But most of the recommendations of the Commissioners remained little more than pious hopes. The Government did set up the Endowed Schools Commission (1869–74) and then merged its work with the Charity Commission (1874–1902). These bodies were invested with extensive powers enabling them to vary the terms of educational trusts. This enabled some of the money to be used for founding schools for girls, for transferring funds from 'dead areas' to where the population now was, and for writing into the new deeds of convenant stipulations about a liberalized curriculum, and the participation in external examinations. Steps were also taken to regularize the government of schools so that scandalous cases of neglect could no longer occur. The long sleep was over, but the awakening was neither complete enough nor active enough to catch up with the increasing social momentum. Indeed, there were clear signs as late as 1902 that far from catching up the secondary schools were falling even further behind, and the Government was at last compelled to intervene much more directly, as they had done with elementary schools in 1870.

Critics of the existing secondary schools had been insisting that this would be necessary for many years. Apart from the gross imbalance of the provision for girls as opposed to boys— and society grew less and less prepared to tolerate this— there were two other strong forces which high-lighted the deficiencies of the secondary schools, and provided a certain amount of pressure to bring them into closer contact with the real needs of the times.

First was the recognition of the importance of technical and scientific education and the beginnings of State intervention in it. At the Great Exhibition in 1851 there were 100 departments in which goods were displayed, and in most of them we took the prizes against foreign competition. But far-sighted people like the Prince Regent could see that all was not well. At the Paris Exhibition of 1867 there were 90 departments, and we only scraped prizes in 10 of them. Public opinion began to be convinced that something must be done or we should rapidly lose our industrial and commercial advantages. So a Royal Commission was set up to consider the matter, and it reported in 1884. It stated quite bluntly that 'the best preparation for technical study is a good modern secondary school of the types of the Manchester Grammar School, the Bedford Modern School, and the Allan Glen's Institution at Glasgow'. The trouble was that there were not enough of these schools, and as 'Private enterprise is clearly inadequate to do all that is required in establishing such schools, we must look for some public measure to supply this, the greatest defect of our educational system.' The Local Government Act of 1888 created County Councils and County Boroughs which were clearly suitable authorities to start this work. They were given the right to levy a penny rate to provide technical education. By a hilarious accident, they also got control of funds called 'Whisky money'. A tax had been imposed on spirits to please temperance interests, and it was intended that the new county and borough councils would use it to buy up publicans' licences to get rid of redundant public houses. But Parliament changed its mind, and resolved instead that it should be used for the provision of scientific and technical education. Separate institutions were either founded or improved and enlarged. But the definition of 'technical' was so wide that it also included the more go ahead secondary schools. This was a great stimulus to them.

The second strong force bringing pressure to bear on the reform of secondary schools was the marked tendency of the elementary schools to forget their supposed station in life, and to show successful experiments in higher education. To start with, the new Board Schools completely revolutionized our traditional idea of what a school should look like. E. R. Robson, the architect of the London School Board, did not build the customary vast hall with tiered seats all round it for all the classes, but rather a hall with separate class-rooms opening from it. This plan became standard, and my own school at the moment is of exactly this style. G. M. Young speaks of the Board Schools as 'those solid, large windowed blocks, which still rise everywhere above the slate roofs of mean suburbs which meant for hundreds of thousands their first glimpse of a life of cleanliness, order, light and air'. Conan Doyle expresses the same idea.

'Look at those big isolated clumps of buildings rising above the slates, like brick islands in a lead coloured sea,' said Sherlock Holmes. 'The Board Schools,' replied Doctor Watson. 'Light houses, my boy,' said Holmes. 'Beacons of the future! Capsules, with hundreds of bright little seeds in each, out of which will spring the wise better England of the future.'

Bright children in the elementary schools raced through the various standards of attainment which they were supposed to take at a far more leisurely rate, and instead of leaving stayed at school and asked for more. Devoted headmasters and staffs gave it to them, even though the Elementary Code said they should do no such thing. Go-ahead School Boards encouraged them to do this. After all, these 'bright little seeds' were the elementary school teachers of tomorrow, or the chief clerks or the under-managers of the day after that. It became customary for the better elementary school to have a group of pupils at the top of it who were doing secondary work. Soon school boards gathered these pupils together in special Central Schools, or made available funds for scholarships with which they could transfer to traditional secondary schools. In this wildly illogical country of ours, it didn't really matter that elementary schools were now doing secondary work, for some secondary schools had been elementary schools for years without ever really admitting it. The important thing was that the work should get done, because even with all hands to the pumps the task was greater than the united resources available. But suddenly the blow fell. On the 26th of July 1899, T. B. Cockerton, the Government Auditor, ruled that the London School Board had no right to spend money given to them to provide elementary education for the provision of further

24

education of this kind. On the 20th of December 1900 he was supported by a judgment in the High Court. Mr. Justice Wills ruled that the idea that School Boards were 'free to teach at the expense of ratepayers to adults and children indiscriminately the higher mathematics, advanced chemistry both theoretical and practical, political economy, art of a kind wholly beyond anything that can be taught to children, French, German, History and I know not what, appears to me to be the *ne plus ultra* of extravagance'. Since the elementary schools were offshoots of the Poor Law, dedicated to providing the barest of minimums as cheaply as possible, 'extravagance' was a heinous offence. But at one stroke of the pen, Mr. Justice Wills had not only got rid of 'extravagance', but also of the educational provisions for 150,000 bright children in the elementary schools of the London area who had voluntarily stayed at school beyond the official leaving age. Throughout the country as a whole, more than 470,000 children were affected, an army of Oliver Twists, who had drunk the thin gruel officially prescribed for them, and were insistently asking for more. Clearly, something had to be done. Sidney Webb wrote a powerful Fabian pamphlet entitled *The Education Muddle and the Way Out*, and after violent political quarrels a way out was found.

Part of the answer had been given, even before Cockerton delivered his bombshell, in the Board of Education Act, 1899. This, for the first time, set up one central education authority. The Education Department hitherto had dealt with elementary education, both that provided in the voluntary or denominational schools, and that provided in the Board Schools. The Science and Art Department had dealt with Technical and Scientific Education, using as its local representatives the fairly recently created County Councils and County Borough Councils. The Charity Commissioners had exercised certain powers over the endowed secondary schools, mainly through their right to review the terms of an endowment. The powers of the Education Department (Elementary), Science and Art Department (Technical), and the Charity Commissioners (Secondary) were now merged into the one Board of Education. Since it was obviously impossible to keep the various types of education separate in watertight compartments, this measure brought about administrative tidiness at the centre. It also did something else. It had long been accepted that elementary schools should be inspected to make sure they were efficient and giving value for money. Now this right of inspection was extended to secondary schools.

The Board of Education may by their officers, or, after taking the advice of the consultative committee hereinafter mentioned, by any university or other organization, inspect any school supplying secondary education and desiring to be so inspected, for the purpose of ascertaining the character of the teaching in the school and the nature of the provisions made for the teaching and health of the scholars.

All very gentlemanly and permissive, but it was the thin end of a very thick wedge. As time passed, the direct effect of this clause on the schools themselves and what went on inside them was tremendously important. It was directly instrumental in bringing in proper secondary education more in tune with the developing needs of the times and the children, and from this point of view was of more importance than the administrative tidiness which attracted most political attention at the time.

Away from the centre, of course, administrative muddle still remained, and the Cockerton Ruling showed how important it was to improve matters throughout the provinces. This was what the Education Act of 1902 set out to do. First it tackled the arrangements for elementary education. The elective School Boards which had been so successful in 'filling in the gaps' that they looked like taking over the entire system, were abolished—and the screams of outraged politicians were deafening. The voluntary and denominational elementary schools, which had found great difficulty in raising the money to keep up with the development in Board Schools, were now to be allowed direct financial assistance from the state—and the screams of their traditional, anti-clerical and nonconformist opponents, who had been enjoying their slow decline, and had been looking forward to their imminent death were terrible to hear. Lloyd George stumped the country with his slogan, 'Rome has been put on the Rates', and 70,000 people were in due course prosecuted for their refusal to pay their rates. The council of every non-county borough with a population of over 10,000, and of every urban district with a population of over 20,000 became the local education authority for elementary education only for that particular district. These were known as the Part III Authorities—a curious and unnecessary complication which was later to disappear. But the really important authorities were the County Councils and the County Borough Councils. They were given control of elementary education in their area, and 'higher education' as well. They were told 'to consider the educational needs of their area and take such steps as seem to them desirable, after consultation with the Board of Education, to supply or aid the supply of education other than elementary and to promote the general co-ordination of all forms of education'. No attempt was made to define what was meant by 'higher education', and this was certainly just as well. The elementary schools and the secondary schools still remained in quite rigid isolation from each other, but the same local body was responsible for their development, and could now with a clear conscience encourage education 'other than elementary' wheresoever and howsoever seemed best. 2,568 School Boards had been replaced by 328 Local Education Authorities with greater powers. Clearly a vast expansion of education was about to take place. It is a curious comment on the ability of politicians to understand what they are about when they meddle with education, that years later, Balfour, who piloted the Education Act of 1902 through the Commons, rather plaintively confessed, 'I did not realize that the Act would mean more expense and more bureaucracy.'

SECONDARY EDUCATION FOR ALL

But you could not have the remarkable development which flowed from the Balfour Act during the next twenty years without a great deal more expense, and a good deal more bureaucracy. Horizons were expanding, and it was coming to be realized that the national system of schools which we were busy creating had a wider function in the field of social engineering than had ever been suspected in the past. Forty years before this, in his evidence to the Newcastle Commission, a future Bishop of Manchester had been able to say:

We must make up our minds to see the last of him as far as the day school is concerned at 10 or 11. We must frame our system of

27

education upon this hypothesis; and I venture to maintain that it is possible to teach a child soundly and thoroughly, in a way that he shall not forget it, all that is necessary for him to possess in the shape of intellectual attainments, by the time that he is ten years old....I have no higher view of the future or possibilities of an English elementary education floating before my eyes than this.

I am quite sure that he would not have ventured to maintain any such ridiculous hypothesis after the 1902 Act. It was coming to be accepted as a truism by then that the state owed to every child a much better opportunity than this. We were, for instance, no longer prepared to tolerate the neglect of the more material aspects of child welfare. Shocked by the evidence of Seebohm Rowntree that over a quarter of the citizens of York could not afford to buy sufficient food to enable them to do a proper day's work, people began to accept the proposition that it was absurd to try to feed a child's mind when its stomach was empty, and so we got the Provision of Meals Act in 1906. As a direct result of the work of Margaret McMillan in Bradford, health centres were set up, and in 1907 education authorities were empowered to provide medical treatment for school children. In 1910, they were also given authority to set up Juvenile Employment Bureaux, to advise boys and girls on their choice of career. More and more aspects of a child's life came to be regarded as the proper province of the local authorities. It was, in fact coming to be gradually accepted that before a school taught anything at all, it had to strive to create an environment and atmosphere conducive to the all-round development of each child, as an individual and as a citizen. There has obviously been a startling change in attitude, forty years and two world wars later, when we find it being laid down in the 1944 Education Act that

It shall be the duty of every local education authority to secure that the facilities for primary, secondary, and further education provided for their area include adequate facilities for recreation and social and physical training. For that purpose a local education authority, with the approval of the Minister, may establish, maintain, and manage, or assist the establishment, maintenance, and management, of camps, holiday classes, playing fields, play centres, and other places (including playgrounds, gymnasia, and swimming baths not appropriated to any school or college) at which facilities for such recreation and for such training are available, and may organize games, expeditions, and other activities, and may defray or contribute towards the expenses thereof.

Schools for heroes to live in! It was enough to set the Rt. Reverend Frazer, sometime Bishop of Manchester, spinning in his grave, but it merely indicates the changing social attitudes and pressures which were having such a powerful effect on our schools.

Society was demanding more, and more efficient, secondary education, and it got it. In fact, from many points of view it would almost be true to say that secondary education as we understand it today started after the 1902 Act. What had existed before was important, and was continued, but suffered a sea change. The successful endowed grammar schools and proprietary schools which had existed before 1902 continued. Less successful endowed schools were taken over by the local authorities and new life breathed into them. Higher sections and selective departments of elementary schools were refashioned as fully-blown secondary schools. All these, plus brand new Municipal and County secondary schools, provided a remarkable expansion in the Secondary field. The 491 schools existing in 1904 had increased to 1,616 in 1925— they had trebled—whilst the pupils in them had nearly quadrupled in the time. The curricula in these schools had altered in many important respects, and methods of teaching had also changed. The buildings were set in pleasant playing fields, usually in desirable suburbs, and the buildings them-selves were completely different architecturally to the old Board Schools. The compact three-storey edifice, with a central hall and class-rooms opening off it (surrounded as likely as not by an asphalt play-ground), was not repeated. Single storey schools were built wherever possible on an open quadrangular principle, so that light and air could get into the class-rooms by the windows on both sides, and amenities such as laboratories, workshops, domestic science rooms, and gymnasia were regarded as the normal necessities. A great many of the children were, of course, fee payers, possibly of quite limited academic ability. But increasing numbers of the pupils had started life in the elementary schools, and had won their way to the secondary school by winning a Minor Scholarship or a Free

Place. They were invariably clever children. So the municipal secondary schools were an interesting mixture of children, widely varied both in academic ability and social class. They were fine institutions. One of them gave me my own start in life, and left me eternally grateful for what it did for me. In fact, nine out of ten people today who instinctively say 'Hands off the Grammar Schools' are referring to the County or Municipal secondary schools set up after the 1902 Act, and not to the ancient endowed grammar schools at all. They were not perfect—no human institution is—and they had one great fault. There were not enough of them; and with the growth in importance of examinations like the School Certificate and later the G.C.E., the demand for places in them was far greater than they could possibly cope with. The expansion continued but it could never keep up with the need.

The fact was that the majority of people still attended the elementary schools, and there was still an uncomfortably large gulf between them and the new secondary schools. I do not mean to suggest that the elementary schools stood still. They did not. Their curricula began to leave the three Rs well behind, and there were great improvements in the general education they provided. They continued to do outstanding work for their brighter children at the newly founded Higher Elementary Schools, Central Schools, and Junior Technical Schools. At least one Nobel Prize-winner, for instance, was a pupil in a higher-grade elementary school. But how many more equally promising pupils failed to make the grade? Was there a pool of untapped talent which was going to waste? There was an uncomfortable feeling that whilst the new secondary schools basked in the limelight, the elementary schools and their pupils were neglected Cinderellas. Financial grants for elementary schools were always smaller and less generous than those for secondary schools. The articles of government invariably gave freedom and independence to secondary schools to manage their own affairs, which was very largely denied to elementary schools. Rates of pay and social standing were higher if you taught in a secondary school. It is easy to see how jealousies and misunderstandings grew up in a teaching profession brutally divided in this way. It is also easy to see that society at large, which was taking a greater interest in providing a richer life for all children, could not permanently tolerate a relatively expensive system for a minority and a comparatively cheap system for the majority. 'Really', they began to say, echoing Colonel Rainborough's remark in Cromwellian times, 'Really I think that the poorest he that is in England hath a life to live as the greatest he. That is for those Puritans as for all true democrats the real meaning of human equality'. Or as Tawney, speaking for the Labour Party in 1922, put it in a book significantly entitled *Secondary Education for All*,

The Labour party is convinced that the only policy which is at once educationally sound and suited to a democratic community is one under which primary education and secondary education are organized as two stages in a single continuous process; secondary education being the education of the adolescent and primary education being education preparatory thereto. Its objective, therefore, is both the improvement of primary education and the development of public secondary education to such a point that all normal children, irrespective of the income, class or occupation of their parents, may be transferred at the age of 'eleven plus' from the primary or preparatory school, and remain in the latter until sixteen. It holds that all immediate reforms should be carried out with that general objective in view, in such a way as to contribute to its attainment. It recognizes that the more secondary education is developed, the more essential will it be that there should be the widest possible variety of type among secondary schools. It therefore looks forward to the time when Central Schools and Junior Technical Schools will be transformed into one part of a system of free and universal education.

Tawney's penultimate sentence is worth rereading for a second or third time, now that party policy has moved on to demanding one comprehensive school for all the children in a district, and it is the blackest of heresies to suggest that what we really need is 'the widest possible variety of type among secondary schools'. But no one, I think, would wish to quarrel with the rest of it even if they cannot endorse the penultimate sentence as heavily as I do.

Certainly the report of the official consultative committee on the *Education of the Adolescent*, published in 1926, and popularly known since as the Hadow Report, did not quarrel with it. Tawney, by the way, was one of the members of this committee. With deceptive modesty it suggested 'the need of some changes of terminology', which the committee felt were 'perhaps not gravely contentious or revolutionary'. They were in fact explosive and dynamic. 'We desire', they said, 'to abolish the word "elementary", and to alter and extend the sense of the word secondary.' The all-age elementary school, in which the majority of the people spent the whole of their school-days, was to be decapitated. The junior section containing children up to the age of 11 was to be a primary school, and at the age of 11 everyone would move off to continue their secondary education elsewhere. This might be in one of the county or municipal schools which had hitherto had a monopoly of the title 'secondary schools', and these schools were now to be known by the name of grammar schools. More probably it would be in a new type of secondary school, for which the Hadow Report suggested the name of 'modern secondary school', or secondary modern as it later became. But it was not sufficient just to change the name. An extra year was to be added to the general school life, to give the new modern secondary schools a chance to plan a full four years' course for their pupils. The staff, too, would need to be more fully trained and more highly qualified, and it was hoped that university graduates after a fourth year of professional training would also elect to teach in these schools. When the majority of children ceased to be taught in elementary schools and were 'transplanted to new ground, and set in a new environment, which should be adjusted, as far as possible, to the interests and abilities of each range and variety', then, the Hadow Committee felt certain, 'they will thrive to a new height and attain a sturdier fibre'. But when? The Hadow reorganizations were started with great enthusiasm, but it all takes time, and it is only in very recent years that we have neared the end of the necessary work. The economic difficulties of the thirties, and the Second World War, have unduly delayed these necessary reforms in some areas, and this has unfortunately soured relations between the different types of secondary schools.

The suggestions of Hadow, Spens, and a host of other official and unofficial reports, together with the strong feeling that we could not afford to win the war and lose the peace, led to the Butler Education Act of 1944. This was a very great act, and made possible as important an advance in public education in this country as has ever been known. The President of the Board of Education, and the Board itself, with their rather vague brief of 'the superintendence of certain matters relating to education in England and Wales', both disappeared. Since, as R. A. Butler pointed out in the debate, the Board had existed since 1900, but had in fact never met, this can have been no great loss. They were replaced by a Minister with much greater and more definite duties. He was to 'promote the education of the people of England and Wales and the progressive development of institutions devoted to that purpose, and to secure the effective execution by local authorities, under his control and direction, of the national policy of providing a varied and comprehensive educational service in every area'. These are very sweeping powers indeed. Notice particularly the words 'comprehensive' and 'varied', and that the word 'varied' is given pride of place. Two Central Advisory Councils (one for England, the other for Wales) were set up to help the Minister. Since there was to be no such thing as elementary education, the Part III Local Authorities which had only had powers to provide elementary education were swept away, and 169 of the then existing 315 Local Education Authorities ceased to exist. It became the statutory duty of the authorities which remained to provide efficient primary and secondary education for every child in their area, and further education for any adult that requires it. To spur on the laggard authorities it was written into the Act that

the schools available for an area shall not be deemed to be sufficient unless they are sufficient in number, character, and equipment to afford for all pupils opportunities for education offering such variety of instruction and training as may be desirable in view of their different ages, abilities, and aptitudes, and of the different periods for which they may be expected to remain at school, including practical instruction and training appropriate to their respective needs.

Within a year of the Act coming into force, every local authority had to prepare and submit to the Minister a 'development plan' showing how they proposed to supply the schools now considered necessary. Voluntary schools were to be given the option of being completely controlled (if they accepted full financial aid from the local authority), or if they were only to be partially maintained they could choose to become 'aided' or 'special agreement' schools. The leaving age was to be raised to 15, and at some future date to 16. Private schools were allowed to continue, but must now register themselves and be open to inspection to prove that they were efficient. Some of the old endowed schools which were receiving public money (now known as the Direct Grant Schools) were allowed to continue charging school fees, but apart from this the payment of school fees in the fully maintained schools of the local authorities was completely abolished. Nursery schools were to be provided in areas where the need existed, and boarding schools where required. The notion of day continuation classes which the Fisher Act of 1918 had attempted to introduce was now resurrected. County Colleges were to be set up, and a child who left school at 15 would be required to attend there for a part of each working week until the age of 18. So no one in this country would lose contact with the educational system until he was 18, and throughout this time there was to be special allowances for milk, meals, clothing, and travelling, so that the poorer children would not be at a disadvantage. It was an omnibus Act, and it is impossible to mention everything contained in its 122 clauses and nine schedules. But two final points are worth making. All secondary schools of whatever type were to be given reasonable independence from the local authority by being given their own Boards of Governors. There was to be a single system of working out the pay of teachers in all secondary schools, whether grammar or secondary modern. It was hoped that the public would rapidly forget their prejudices, and give complete parity of esteem to all types of secondary school. We had at long last arrived. We had now a fully comprehensive system of secondary schools, varied in type and circumstances, but united in providing what the varied ages, abilities, and aptitudes of their pupils required. We had now got Secondary Education for all, and one had only to look at the Statute Book to prove it. What then seems to be the trouble?

34

SECOND THOUGHTS

The trouble was that there was an enormous gap between the promised land of the Act and the harsh realities of the existing world. Cautious pessimists pointed out that it would be twenty or thirty years before this gap could be eliminated; but the way things turned out proved that these cautious pessimists were extremely optimistic to expect complete satisfaction in any thing like this time. First of all, there was the question of building enough schools of the right type. This would have been a long and difficult process at the best of times, but there were additional complications. During the Second World War, over 5,000 schools—accommodation for something like 300,000 pupils—had been either seriously damaged or destroyed by enemy action. Since even before the war it had been estimated that four out of every five elementary schools were so out of date that they needed rebuilding, and the neglect of the war years had made this situation even worse, some idea of the amount of rebuilding needed to cover basic necessities becomes obvious, quite apart from that needed for creating a new and better environment for all. Moreover, a steep and continuing rise in the birth rate increased the numbers of children in school by about a third, whilst the number of children staying voluntarily at school beyond the age of fifteen also increased in a quite dramatic way. So did the mobility of the population, as new areas developed and old areas declined. At this time, too, it was necessary to build hospitals, factories, houses, and roads, at a time when the country was staggering from one economic crisis to another. With the best will in the world it was just not possible to give high enough priority to school building to enable the mammoth task to be completed in a reasonable time. A large building programme was launched and maintained, as each area pressed on as best it could with its development plan. By 1964 6,500 new schools had been built, and the quality of their facilities was most impressive. Moreover the emphasis was on the building of replacements for the old elementary sector—in other words, new primary schools and secondary moderns rather than grammar schools, whose buildings tended to be neglected, and to become increasingly crowded and out of date. But however hard the authorities

35

tried, in far too many cases the public noticed that little appeared to have changed except the notice board at the gate, that the old buildings remained in use and that the children condemned to live in them were not getting the amenities of a proper secondary education. An official report in 1962 estimated that it would cost £1,368 million to bring the maintained primary and secondary schools in England and Wales up to modern standards of accommodation, which was seventeen times the whole of the current annual school building programme.

Middle-class parents voted with their feet, and sent their children to private schools; one of the curious and unexpected by-products of the 1944 Act being that it led to an expansion of the private sector rather than to the reverse, and saved from extinction many minor and pseudo-public schools which were on the verge of bankruptcy. Working-class parents had, however, little option but to send their children to the State schools, and became more and more embittered at what they considered to be the rank injustice of it all. After all, few people in this country have any interest in education as such, or care twopence for development plans and prophecies of what things will be like in the sweet by and by. But they are passionately anxious that their little John and Mary shall have a good start in life—at least as good as the children next door— if possible a good deal better—but under no circumstances any worse. And the plain fact of the matter was that at the moment in time that John and Mary needed them the appropriate schools just were not there.

Nor were the teachers. Immediately after the war, fifty-five country houses or disused military establishments were set up as Emergency Training Colleges for Teachers. The intention was to capture for the teaching profession men and women whose war-time experience had fitted them for, and interested them in, teaching. They unearthed a great many first class teachers, and it was a criminal folly to close down so many of the colleges when the first wave of demobilization had passed. Since then there have been many attempts to increase the supply of teachers—partially nullified by the changing social pattern of young women leaving the profession after increasingly early marriage, and by the many other opportunities of interesting employment opened up to young men in our modern world. It is true that the numbers trained have markedly increased, and the quality of their training has also improved. In 1960, the normal period of training in a Teachers' Training College, for instance, was increased from two to three years; and the broader horizons of these colleges have been indicated by the recent change of name to Colleges of Education, and they are now able to present their better students for a Bachelor of Education degree. I would not wish to decry the efforts of the people concerned in producing more and better teachers, but the fact is that they have been too little and too late. In fact, education in the least attractive schools in the least attractive areas would have broken down altogether had not the Ministry of Education imposed a system of teacher quotas on the local authorities. Each authority is told the maximum number of teachers it should employ in its schools, the figures being so arranged that the teaching force is spread out more evenly over the country as a whole than it would otherwise be. Teachers, in fact, are rationed.

No political party has suggested that it would abolish this administrative device if it came to power—because it would be obvious lunacy to do so until the supply of teachers was more nearly adequate to the need. Nevertheless the gravity of being compelled to ration teachers whilst you are at the same time demanding wholesale expansion of the education services cannot be over-emphasized. How could the schools provide secondary education for all in these circumstances? Yet the public expected them to do so, and were bitterly disappointed. They clamoured more and more to get their children into the grammar schools—the old secondary schools with a good local reputation—whether or not their children were really capable of profiting from the education offered there. But there was a shortage of these schools nationally, and the provision of them varied most alarmingly from one area to another. The national average was by 1956 just over 20 per cent, but in some places in England it was as low as 10 per cent or as high as 40 per cent, and in parts of Wales reached 60 per cent. The opportunities this gave for social discontent were obvious. Moreover, the clamour to get into a grammar school had the unfortunate effect that it became fashionable to denigrate the secondary

37

modern schools. 'Run away to sea rather than go to a secondary modern', advised one learned academic, who was probably as ignorant of what went on in the one place as he was of what went on in the other. But the fact remained that 'parity of esteem' between secondary modern schools and grammar schools was not granted. It showed a complete lack of human understanding to expect that it would be—at least not till after twenty or thirty years of bitter struggle had allowed the secondary modern schools to prove that they really deserved it. There is a moral here for local authorities who take old school buildings and existing staff and declare that overnight they have become fine new comprehensives. The public will not believe them until they have proved it.

Handicapped as it was by shortage of buildings and teachers, would it be true to say that the Butler Act did not work? It would be truer to say that it was never tried. Two of its extremities never got out of the Statute Book. To all intents and purposes, nursery schools just failed to materialize in the way and the numbers that had been expected. Yet in terms of social justice it was vital that they should. It is precisely at this early stage of his life that a child from a limited or deprived home most needs the stimulus of a nursery school to enrich his social experience, and to give him a fair start in life. By the time he is old enough to enter the infant school, a great deal of damage has been done, and he is already in many cases a 'second class citizen'. Nor did the County Colleges materialize either. They were expected to provide part-time education from 15 to 19 for all those who were not in full-time education. Imagine the powerful effect this would have had on the problems of juvenile delinquency, and in providing real links between school days and the fuller responsibilities of the adult world. In 1959 the Central Advisory Council for Education made a full-scale report on the education of children from 15 to 18, which came to be known as the Crowther Report. They had been asked to consider it in relation to the changing social and individual needs of our society, and the needs of its individual citizens. The first two sentences of their Report are quite shattering in their implications: 'This report is about the education of English boys and girls aged from 15 to 18. Most of them are not being educated.'

38

To judge by some of the wilder and less well-informed newspaper reports the same might well have been true of boys and girls aged from 11 to 15 in our secondary modern schools. But fortunately we have something a good deal more reliable to go on, and from this source a completely different picture starts to emerge. In 1963 the Central Advisory Council for Education produced another full-scale report on the education of children from 13 to 16 of average and less than average ability. The majority of these children (though by no means all) were in secondary modern schools. The Report—officially entitled *Half our Future*, but rapidly christened 'The Newsom Report' because of the name of its chairman—contained a great many suggestions of what needed to be done before we could start to feel satisfied that these children were getting proper secondary education. We will need to examine these suggestions later, but cannot escape from looking immediately at what the Advisory Council in the first sentence of its Report says is 'the most important of our recommendations, implicit in the whole of our report, even though it will not be found specifically in the text'. They were concerned that these young people

should receive a greater share of the national resources devoted to education than they have done in the past, and by resources we do not mean solely finance, although this is important. . . . We are concerned that there should be a change of attitude towards these young people not only among many of those who control their education but among the public at large and this cannot be achieved solely, if at all, by administrative action. It involves a change of thinking, and even more a change of heart.

A great social experiment, which is what the secondary modern schools were, is doomed to failure from the start unless society is fully aware of what the experiment is all about, and is prepared to be tolerant and understanding of the very real difficulties involved. By and large, society has not been prepared to be either tolerant or understanding. Yet to attempt to judge the success or failure of secondary modern schools (and also of the new comprehensives, don't forget) until they have had a spell of twenty or so years with reasonable facilities, is premature and unfair. No amount of 'sloganizing' or banner

39

waving, or wholesale reorganization on yet another administrative pattern, will make these fundamental educational difficulties disappear.

We cannot stress too strongly that the solution to these problems is not necessarily to be found by a reorganization of the present pattern of secondary education. However large or small the school, whether it is one sex or co-educational, however wide its range of intellectual ability, the problems peculiar to the pupils we have been considering still remain to be solved.

In a later chapter we will have to look at the painfully difficult ways that comprehensive schools will have to take to set about their solution.

Meanwhile, the most surprising thing to emerge from the Newsom Report—and this has not had the attention it deserved—was the sound, steady advances which have been made by the teachers in secondary modern schools, against almost impossible odds, towards some kind of a solution to these educational problems. Never mind what the papers said, or what your own prejudices may be; the Newsom Committee carried out a careful and meticulous survey to see what the exact position was.

Although this report is about the academically less successful (they state), it is a success story that we have to tell. . . . Today's average boys and girls are better at their books than their predecessors half a generation ago. There are reasons to expect that their successors will be better still. . . . Between 1953 and 1961 there has been a general improvement in standards in which all occupational groups have shared. There is also, and it is this which is particularly important, a tendency for the lower occupational groups to show a somewhat greater improvement than the higher ones. This is a first instalment of what can be expected as manual workers become increasingly familiar with what secondary education offers their children.

Quite apart from what the alarmists said, therefore, this careful factual survey revealed a picture of rising averages. Steady progress was obviously being made. But it was also apparent from the survey that there was a marked contrast between the attainments of children in different schools. For instance, if your child was lucky enough to go to a good secondary modern school he had a marked advantage over a child going to a poor secondary modern school, since the group average reading age in the one could be up to five and three-quarter years ahead of the other. Again, the survey attempted to discover the effect the neighbourhood exerted on the quality of the education given in the secondary modern schools within its area, and found that it was most significant. Of course, you could find good and bad schools in most neighbourhoods. Nevertheless there was a marked pattern of better attainment in a good neighbourhood than in a bad neighbourhood which was not accidental. A good neighbourhood was defined as a mixture of rural area or urban area, possibly with a council estate or a new town, but certainly with a high proportion of owner-occupied houses. A bad or problem neighbourhood was an industrial area of bad housing with a high concentration of social problems. The group average reading age between these two neighbourhoods might be expected to vary by up to twelve months. A specifically slum area showed a gap of an additional year in the average reading age between itself and a bad or problem area. This must surely give cause for great concern, particularly now that we are committed to the wholesale introduction of comprehensive schools, when it is envisaged that all children in a neighbourhood will attend the same school. This may in many cases accentuate even more the inequalities of neighbourhoods, and lead to further social injustice rather than less.

But the simple point of the Newsom Report must not be missed by straying too far away from it into details. There never are enough buildings or enough teachers, but it is surprising how much can be done, and is being done, to get over these difficulties in schools of all kinds. 'We have been impressed', says the Newsom Report, 'by what the schools have achieved since the concept of secondary education for all was initiated.' The Newsom Report concentrated on direct and practical suggestions to the schools on how to achieve more, making it pretty clear to politicians, administrators, and the general public how they could help. The members of the Newsom Committee concentrated on 'the kernel of the problem, and have not discussed, as some people would have expected us to do, the organization of the secondary school pattern throughout the country'. But some people, more people, and with ever more insistence, did want to discuss an even more radical change in the pattern of secondary schools. They wanted to abolish the 11+, and to get rid of all three types of secondary school—grammar, secondary technical, and secondary modern—replacing them by the comprehensive school.

It is curious that the two most contentious things to arise as a result of the Butler Act are not even mentioned in it. Though insisting that children must be educated in schools which would vary according to their age, ability, and aptitude, it does not say what those varying types of school should be. But most local authorities worked to the tripartite pattern as envisaged in the Hadow and Spens Reports, and created grammar, technical, or modern schools. Technical schools tended to be least popular with local authorities, and the expansion here was less great than might have been expected. Perhaps this was because it became increasingly difficult to decide at the early age of eleven whether a child was 'technical' as opposed to 'grammar' or 'modern'. For the second thing which was not mentioned in the Act, but was left for the local authorities to solve as best they could, was how one was to select a child for the appropriate school. Each authority had to work this one out for itself, and no two solutions were exactly the same. Usually the 11+ (as it came to be known in all areas however it varied) contained some mixture or other of three things. There was some test of the child's attainment in basic matters such as English and Mathematics. There was some consideration given to his record in the primary school, and what his primary teachers thought of his academic potentialities. The child was also given an objective test of his intelligence, which was supposed to give an unbiased, uncorruptible, and unchangeable indication of how well, or how badly he would tackle academic work.

There had been fumblings towards an 11+ Test of this nature long before the 1944 Act. In 1913 the L.C.C. had set up the first child guidance clinic in the country, and by case study and statistical analysis Sir Cyril Burt had shown how useful psychological tests could be to help diagnose the educational requirements of dull, defective, delinquent, and neurotic children. During the First World War the American Army used group tests to sort out its recruits, and it seemed clear that suitably modified tests would be useful in the junior scholarship examinations to choose boys and girls from elementary schools for transfer to grammar schools, and they were adopted by Bradford for this purpose in 1919. By 1923 they were extended in a startling and interesting manner. The Northumberland Education Committee were very concerned at the large number of children in this county who were never even entered for the junior scholarship examination, and anxious to stop the waste of talent which was obviously occurring. They therefore devised a set of group tests for all the children in the area, which was so successful in bringing to light unexpected talent in out of the way villages and unfashionable schools that it soon spread to other areas. The Hadow Committee had also made a report on *Psychological Tests of Educable Capacity*, so there was a certain amount of experience and guidance that the authorities could draw on when devising their first 11 + Tests.

But not enough. A little knowledge was to prove a very dangerous thing. These progressive and enlightened people were storing up an unsuspected load of trouble for themselves. Let us try, if we can, to get beneath and behind the emotional and political dust-storm which quickly surrounded their heads, and see quietly and objectively what the weaknesses of the 11 + were, as opposed to what its opponents at times said they were. Let us not forget in passing that, imperfect instrument though it might be, it was not always wrong, and it had its part to play in the greatest expansion of secondary education amongst the children of the poor that this country had so far seen. The steady measured tones of an extract from *Procedures for the Allocation of Pupils in Secondary Education*, published by the National Foundation for Educational Research in 1963, helps us to do this admirably. I quote it in full, as it is important if one wants to get at the truth of the matter to study this piece of genuine and honest research with the utmost care. What it does not say is as important as what it does say. It is the perfect antidote to a great deal of fevered and tendentious clap-trap which tends to get talked on this subject by passionate adherents on both sides of the fence:

There are however certain criticisms which can be made on educational and psychological grounds of the present system of allocation in most of its varieties. These may be summed up as follows:

(a) The age of eleven is too early definitively to force what amounts to a pre-vocational choice; some 'rejected' children show that they are able to follow academic courses, while some 'accepted' children fail either to stay at school or to pass the G.C.E. examinations;

(b) the rhythms of physical and psychological development may be associated with intellectual growth; they differ widely in the pre-pubertal and pubertal period; there is some evidence that early developers, particularly girls, may have an advantage over late developers because of an accelerated mental growth, an advantage which disappears later;

(c) the whole idea of a single decisive occasion is calculated to cause anxiety to parents, children and teachers, accidents of health, an 'off-day' and similar fortuitous circumstances may adversely affect a child's chances out of all proportion to their real importance;

(d) any examination or test provokes teachers and/or parents to attempt to prepare children for it; the 11+ procedures involving tests have a 'backwash' effect on the primary schools, and this is widely held to cramp educational initiative, by defining the syllabus in the fields tested and by giving them so prominent a place in the curriculum as to reduce the time given to other subjects not tested;

(e) because of differences in the proportion of grammar school places, opportunities differ from locality to locality and between boys and girls;

(f) there is also some evidence which suggests that present tests (and even more so, most other examining techniques) tend to favour 'convergent' (analytic or reproductive) thinking rather than 'divergent' (creative or productive) thinking.

The first three of these objections have force only: (i) if the choice is irrevocable; (ii) if the opportunities offered by the different types of education after eleven differ seriously in quality and in ultimate economic value (as distinct from content); and (iii) if later progression to forms of further education depends mainly upon the previous pattern of schooling.

The pity of it is that the authorities did not know all this twenty or thirty years ago, but it is always easy to be wise after the event.

In the intervening years they had been working busily away

refining and modifying their tests until from some points of view they reached a standard of precision greater than that of any other public examination in this country. But for reasons set out in the previous paragraph these tests were bound to be fallible, and with the entire future of their child apparently at stake, parents in the long run would not put up with anything this side of infallibility. Authorities spread the tests over a period of time, and introduced all sorts of safeguards to make sure that a child was not unfairly penalized for having an off day. Arrangements were made for children to take the test again at 12+, at 13+, and for them to transfer to the sixth form of grammar schools at 16+, or to continue with their studies at the local technical college. It was not true that the future of any single child was decided for all time on the result of his performance in one examination on one day of his eleventh year. Examples of 11+ 'failures' who later achieved outstanding academic success—usually produced to show how fallible the system was—were also illustrations that the 'second chance' was a reality and not a myth. But it remained a myth just the same for far too many children. They had fallen at the first fence so clearly jumping was not for them. They had been classed as failures, so clearly that was what they were, and what they ought to remain. There grew up a powerful and pernicious folk-lore that insisted that there were no second chances, and this took such a hold on the mind of the public at large that the myth became the reality.

This caused genuine concern, and a widespread feeling of injustice and gerrymandering. The more sensational press and a good deal of unworthy political propaganda saw that plenty of oil was poured on the flames. After all, what father was prepared to admit that his child's lack of success in the attainment tests in English and Arithmetic was due to hereditary dullness, and if he did, what mother was prepared to agree with him, and confirm that their swan was in fact a goose? It was easier to point out that some schools made a better job of preparing their children for these tests than others, and that your child had been penalized for the deficiencies of his primary school, and not for his own shortcomings—and occasionally the parents were right. Could the parents be convinced that the report of the primary school on the child's potentialities was fair and above board? Most certainly not. They are, by and large, possibly the most accurate and reliable test of all, but it is difficult to convince a disappointed parent that this is so. Then how about the objective intelligence test and the I.Q.? Was not this conclusive? Unfortunately it was not. Verbal reasoning tests of this kind tended to favour the child who came from the sort of home where he had been used to hearing such verbal reasoning taking place between articulate and educated parents, and tended to penalize the child who had not had the advantages of such a home. Possibly they did test something of importance, but it was not an abstract entity which could be labelled Intelligence with a capital I, and which remained constant. There were many other valuable qualities which they did not even start to measure. Statistical evidence was produced to show that whatever the original intention had been, the system was operating unfairly. The unfairness was weighing much more heavily on the children of the working classes than on the middle classes. Curious that a clever administrative device to close the doors of the grammar schools to the dull middle-class child whose parents could pay the fees, and to open them to the bright working-class child whose parents could not, should itself be branded with the stigma of class distinction. But it was. And this made certain that sooner or later it would have to go, but left it far from certain what would take its place.

To my mind, what is needed is more selection and not less, more light and less darkness, and the advent of the comprehensive school will certainly increase it rather than reduce it. We are just on the threshold of a tremendous increase of diagnostic aptitude tests, which will be of the utmost value to a child in helping it to decide which courses it would be best for it to take, and of enormous assistance to the school in seeing that each child gets the appropriate treatment. These tests will start as early as the infant school, and will be repeated in different forms at the important decision-making times right throughout its school life. The real weakness of the 11 + as we have known it was that it pretended to be such a diagnostic test, and was not. It produced an order of merit at a moment in time which was very accurate indeed—but it assumed, wrongly, that this order would remain constant for the next five or six

years. It purported to judge which children would profit
from an academic education, and which would be better suited
for a more practical kind of schooling. In the majority of cases
it produced adequate evidence on which the right decision could
have been made. But in fact, the decision was finally made on
other grounds entirely. There were only x grammar school
places available in each area, and if more children than this
did well in the 11+ they found themselves in secondary
modern schools notwithstanding. Since the places available
in grammar schools varied widely from area to area this produced an intolerable situation. The 11 + was in fact a rationing
device to share out the scarce commodity of secondary education,
and not a diagnostic test at all. But the wise thing to do was
not to abolish it, but to increase the supply of the scarce commodity so that rationing was no longer necessary, and proper
treatment could be given to every child after a proper diagnosis
of its needs had been made.

Wise authorities have been working desperately towards
this over the years. They have done everything possible to
bridge the gap between the grammar and secondary modern
schools which still exists in the public mind. Since it is the fact
that a certain number of pupils in a secondary modern school
might equally well be in the grammar school, G.C.E. streams
have been started in secondary modern schools for these
children, and arrangements made for them to transfer to
grammar school sixth forms for 'A' Level work, or to technical
colleges for the appropriate advanced examinations. The C.S.E.
has now been introduced as an examination more suitable
in every way for these schools, and has met with an enthusiastic
response. Some authorities, notably Bolton, Derby, Brighton,
and the Isle of Wight developed 'school bases', embodying
grammar, technical, and modern schools as separate entities,
but sharing common facilities on the same site. Some established
bilateral schools—grammar technical or technical modern—
in which it was possible for children to change courses as their
potentialities increased or decreased. Leicestershire experimented with junior non-selective high schools for children
whose parents were prepared to keep them at school until the
age of 16 at least. Other authorities, notably the L.C.C.,
Birmingham, Coventry, and the West Riding were pioneers

in building very large schools to cater for all the needs of all
the children of secondary school age in a district. These were
the comprehensives. Were these the final answer? Clearly the
educational world was in a state of turmoil. When since 1870
and beyond has it been in any other state?

3

The Changes

Instead of generalizing about the country as a whole, it may be helpful if I describe the experiences of one working headmaster, lost in the Alice-in-Wonderland world of Comprehensive Reorganization. 'Man is the only animal that laughs and weeps', said Hazlitt, 'for he is the only animal that is struck by the difference between what things are and what they might have been.' I have tried in the last three chapters to give you, not only an idea of 'what things are', but of the long, hard, bitter struggle which has been necessary to reach this state of affairs, however imperfect it may be. You must take it from me that it is requiring remarkable efforts to maintain the present position, and in addition to maintaining it we are managing to advance slowly and surely all along the line. Now if there were some instant solution to all our problems, I would be the first to welcome it, but natural caution makes one hesitate to lose all one has worked for in what may turn out to be the vain pursuit of a will-o'-the-wisp. One needs to be very sure and very certain, and certainty and surety are just not to be found in negotiations of this kind. Everybody knows 'why' it should be done, and can tell you 'when' it is going to happen, but 'how' is another matter. As you pin them down to detail the truth finally comes out. There is no such thing as The Comprehensive School—it is a bloodless abstraction which does not exist. Every one founded so far is different, and every one founded in the future will differ in some respects from its immediate predecessor. Some of them will be better than

49

anything we now know, and some will be a good deal worse. In other words, there will continue to be good schools and bad schools in the future, just as there have been in the past, and it will be the quality and number of the teachers running them which will decide into which category they fall. As I have shown, it was felt by many that a solution had been found in 1870, in 1902, and in 1944; and the solutions of the 1960s are likely to be no more permanently satisfying than their predecessors. During the last traumatic years I have had Hazlitt's words ringing in my ears, as I have laughed and wept by turns, and sometimes found myself doing both at the same time.

Does this mean that I want to keep everything as it is, and am opposed to the idea of progress? Nothing could be further from the truth. I do not see how any headmaster in any of our state schools can possibly take up such an attitude, or even be accused of doing so. Have we not been committed since 1944 to providing 'secondary education for all', suitable to the 'age, ability, and aptitude' of every child? Was not the Minister charged in that year with the specific duty of securing 'the effective execution by local authorities, under his control and direction, of the national policy of providing a varied and comprehensive educational service in every area'? Can we possibly call a halt to progress until this ideal has become reality? The painful way ahead was charted in the Crowther and Newsom Reports, and I know no teacher who is not anxious to follow the path to better things. But when one is personally responsible for the future of a thousand boys, and appreciates and is proud of the efforts of one's predecessors over the last fifty years which have made the school what it is, one looks for certain guarantees. It would be complete dereliction of duty to do otherwise.

In common with most other headmasters in a similar position, I found myself asking for a decalogue of guarantees, ten commanding points on which I wanted reassurance. Firstly, was the proposed change likely to improve the opportunities of all children, the clever as well as the less clever; or did it purport to improve the lot of some by making worse the lot of others? Robbing Peter to pay Paul is not wise, and levelling down instead of up can be quite disastrous. You see

I am certain we are not doing enough for the duller child, and equally certain that we could do even more for the brighter child than we do. I want a definite improvement all along the line. Secondly, does the proposed change give real weight to the parent's views on choice of school for his child? A point was made of this in the 1944 Act, but it has been whittled away by administrative action ever since. When no real choice is given apathy or rebellion quickly grows. The school is off to a flying start if parent and child feel that they are connected with it because they want to be, and not because they had it wished on them. Besides, it is a fallacy to talk about State Schools being free. Parents pay for them through rates and taxes, and have a right to reasonable choice, however wrong-headed their choice may appear to be. Thirdly, does it respect existing good schools, of whatever kind, and make certain that if any good schools have to lose their identity they are replaced by something which can be shown to be at least as good? There are not enough good schools around to allow us to carve them up with impunity. They take time to grow and develop, and time is a commodity that we have not much of in this rapidly moving world of ours. Fourthly, does it make full use of all the schools that have traditionally served the area and given satisfaction to people in the past? Denominational schools, direct grant schools, and some private and independent schools come into this category. Fifthly, is it being sensible about buildings? If these are widely separated it is difficult to run a school of any kind, and almost impossible to create an integrated and closely knit community, which is what a comprehensive school is supposed to be. Sixthly, does it take sufficient notice of the fact that education is a continuous process, which should not be interrupted unnecessarily or chopped into arbitrary pieces? In particular, though special facilities are always necessary for a sixth form, it is a fallacy to remove it completely from the school and imagine that nothing has changed. Both sixth form and main school lose many important things, not least the ability of sixth form teachers to make contact with boys and girls when they are still very junior. Seventhly, does it make proper use of staff? Teachers recruited for their abilities in one direction are not always or necessarily equally suited for a different type of work. Eighthly, does it make it difficult for children moving from another part of the country to be fitted into the area schools? Ninthly, quite apart from the social benefits which its advocates hope it will bring, does it bring sufficiently big educational benefits to justify the money involved being spent in this direction, and not on some other project, such as improving the primary schools or adding to the supply of teachers? Tenthly, are its advocates prepared to discuss it thoroughly with the teachers who have to work it, and the parents whose confidence it is essential to gain?

Each of these ten points is important in the difficult task of assessing whether this is simply change for the sake of change, or real progress. They put in a nutshell the case of the maintained grammar schools, and with varying degrees of success they have been urged up and down the country during the comprehensive controversy. They would seem to be matters of simple common-sense, and applicable to all other schools as well. Indeed, there would seem to be nothing here which the strongest advocate of comprehensive schools could not also accept. It is remarkable then that it was so often misrepresented and misunderstood, and that so much bitterness arose.

Because behind all the wordy battles of the extreme protagonists on both sides lay the unescapable reality that they would have to settle for a compromise—good, bad, or indifferent— in the end. This was surely the blinding truism of Forster in 1870, and the lesson had been repeated with sickening regularity every time education had become a bone of political contention since that time. The nature of the compromise finally arrived at in any area, after a completely unnecessary amount of blood, sweat, and tears, had in most cases already been decided by decisions taken many years before with quite other circumstances in mind—decisions about bricks, and mortar, and school sites, and housing estates, and factories, and roads, and declining or increasing centres of population. Looked at from this point of view the national predicament can be stated with extreme simplicity. The 5,900 or so state secondary schools which we now possessed were of varying age and adaptability, but you could not escape from the fact they held an average of just under 500 pupils each. Nor could you side-step the fact that you would have to go on using these buildings for many years to come, and that groups of children of this size were just not large enough to meet the needs of comprehensive schools. Locally, all kinds of historical accidents, some man made, some completely beyond his control, had combined both to complicate the administrative conundrum still further, and also to dictate the only viable solution, if there was one, and you had the wit to spot it. That is why it is important to realize that the early chapters of this book do not just record the outlines of dim and dusty battles of the past, dead and gone beyond recall, but rather remind us of the presence in our midst of ghostly but powerful and lively 'supernatural' influences, shaping and fashioning our future however much we like to pretend that we are free agents and will have no dealings with them.

When Hitler's bombs rained down on Coventry, for instance, spreading complete devastation throughout the twisted medieval alleys of that fine old city, they created a crisis which only the boldest and most imaginative planning could hope to cope with, if an educational phoenix was ever to rise from the flames. When the shadow factories of war-time lived on into the post-war world, and became the growth points for tremendous industrial expansion in peace-time, and high wage-rates attracted a flood of workers from all parts of the United Kingdom and beyond, the crisis hardened into a semi-perpetual and constantly increasing challenge. There was a quite phenomenal increase in population. The secondary school population trebled between 1946 and 1960. What, then, were the City Fathers to do when on top of all this they were also faced with the additional demands of the 1944 Act for 'secondary education for all'? They could have decided to build a few more grammar schools and a great many more secondary modern schools, but this seemed to them to be out of tune with their interpretation of the spirit of the 1944 Act. As they had to build something, and build it fast, they were one of the first of the Local Authorities to decide that all new secondary schools built by them would be on the comprehensive pattern, providing courses for children of differing aptitudes from the age of 11 to eventually 18. By 1965 they had established eight of these purpose-designed schools, and though only two of them had been fully developed, they already accommodated

9,000 of the total secondary school population of 20,400. Shades of the religious controversies of 1870 and 1902, there were also a small Church of England comprehensive school, and a group of 'campus' type Roman Catholic schools accommodating a further 3,400 pupils (all built since 1953). Now, however doctrinaire you may be, in circumstances as acute as these you cannot afford to neglect school places in any kind of school. The Authority therefore continued to maintain two grammar schools for 1,100 girls, and to pay the fees for 1,000 boys at the two Direct Grant grammar schools, it being a curiosity of Coventry that it had never built any grammar schools of its own for boys, but had been happy to rely on two ancient foundations. The remainder of its pupils (approximately 5,800) were in 14 secondary modern schools. Now here is a pioneer city which is already accommodating half of its secondary school children in purpose-built all-through comprehensive schools, and you might suppose that it would be comparatively simple to press on and complete the other half of the task. You would be wrong. Conscious of the tremendous difficulties of moving onward from this 'mixed economy', the Education Committee appointed a working party in 1962 to re-examine completely the organization of secondary education within the city. I do not wish to follow this development in detail—simply to make the point that it started its deliberations where circumstances dictated that it should start them, that the starting-point to a large extent determined its final conclusions, and that the starting-point was quite different from that of almost any other city or county area you care to mention.

Take Cardiff, for instance, completely at random. There had been a strong tradition of providing separate opportunities for bright children here, going right back to 1885 when a Higher Grade elementary school was set up. Since then eight grammar schools (known locally as High Schools), two voluntary Roman Catholic grammar schools, and a technical high school had been established. A number of places were available at a Direct Grant grammar school for girls, and this meant that there was grammar school provision for something like 30 to 33 per cent of the pupils. There was no 'Hadow' reorganization in Cardiff until 1950, which meant that boys and girls who did not move on to high schools had the whole of their education in elementary schools which they had entered at the age of seven. There was therefore a man-sized job after 1950 to rush through the reorganization of secondary modern schools, which had far too often to be established in old and unsatisfactory elementary school premises. The effect of the increased 1947 birth-rate hit the secondary schools in 1958, and it meant a reduction in grammar school selection from 30 to 20 per cent unless something was done about it. Instead of building an additional grammar school, it was decided to establish G.C.E. streams in post-war secondary modern schools. In the same year the first serious steps were made to review the entire organization of secondary education in the city in order that the 11 + examination might be abolished. The large, all-through, 11 to 18 comprehensive schools were first considered, and visits paid to Coventry, Birmingham, London and the West Riding to see them in action. The heavy capital cost of introducing them to Cardiff ruled them out, and some consideration was given to other possibilities, including some kind of two-tier system as in Leicestershire. In 1963 there was a further review of all the alternatives, and it was decided that from September 1965 secondary education in Cardiff would be organized in two stages, but that the organization would be markedly different from the Leicestershire plan, since in Cardiff the predominant thought has been to maintain and enhance the traditions of highly respected existing schools. Somewhat similar thinking was leading to rather similar conclusions in Doncaster, which will be discussed later in another context.

The situation in Bristol, on the other hand, was quite different again. The important point here is that their revised Development Plan of 1951 modified the earlier proposals of the 1946 Development Plan (which called for only two kinds of secondary school, not three), leaving the decision as to how secondary education was to be organized on each site much more open; whilst at the same time the sites ear-marked for new secondary schools were very large—30, 40, or 50 acres each. The idea was that sites of this size gave the authority the necessary flexibility to build whatever type of school or groups of schools it chose when the time came for it to build, whereas a larger number of smaller sites would have tied its hands. Moreover, a large, powerful, secondary organization, concentrated in one place, and with all the resources of buildings and playing fields, would make an admirable 'community centre' for the otherwise amorphous new housing estates which were about to be built, so large areas were reserved for this purpose, right in the centre of the communities which were about to be built. As one community developed, so did the other. The fascinating thing is that as these new schools grew and developed, approximating each year nearer and nearer to comprehensive schools, they did so in quite different ways, developing their own special strengths connected with the special demands of their own areas. In May 1963, the education committee appointed a Development Plan Sub-Committee which met regularly through a period of about fifteen months to plan the way ahead. The Long Term Plan they decided on is simple and straightforward—unduly and disarmingly so. There were seventeen comprehensive schools in existence at the moment, accommodating more than 60 per cent of the maintained secondary school population. Twenty-six comprehensive schools would be sufficient to cover the whole city, so one simply needed to build nine extra comprehensive schools on the remaining sites, assimilating the seven maintained grammar schools into these new buildings, and the job was done. But if you have ever tried to drink a yard of ale you will know that the first couple of feet or so go down with the greatest of ease; whilst the last few inches are the very devil, and really do test 'flexibility'. With all the luck in the world, it will be ten or fifteen years before this simple final solution can possibly come about, and so an extremely complicated and contentious Short Term Plan had also to be worked out. This caused tremendous controversy. There are seven Direct Grant grammar schools in Bristol, two of them Roman Catholic schools, all enjoying a high reputation; and for many years the education committee have paid the fees of half the entrants in some of these schools and a quarter in the others. Taking into account these and the local authority grammar schools, 30 per cent of the eleven-year-old age group is 'extracted' for grammar school courses; and it is easy to see that if this is allowed to continue it can affect the quality of the intake of the comprehensive schools. The local authority grammar schools must therefore be 'assimilated', say the supporters of the plan; for 'assimilated' read 'destroyed' say its opponents. From September 1965, said the education committee, we cease to send any more new free-placers to the Direct Grant schools; and though statistically the numbers concerned were small, parents are not in the habit of regarding their own children as statistics, and the outcry was loud and long. The timing of change is almost more important than the change itself, and it is ironic that an authority with the wisdom to give itself all the flexibility in the world for its building operations should have proved so inflexible in this respect, and should have stirred up for itself even more inflexible opposition to its schemes than it might otherwise have done. Again, I do not wish to bring these developments right up to date, simply to indicate how the starting-points influence the direction which they take at a later stage.

And if these vary from city to city, then the same is true of every county area, and one example of the many will have to suffice. Before the war the County of Durham had suffered terribly in the economic depression, and had been able to spend far less on education than it would have liked. One result was that the percentage of grammar school places was lower than the national average, and this in a part of the world where it had been burnt into the minds of the thinking members of the working classes that to get their children a grammar school education was the only sure way to save them from the dole queues and the social misery which inexorably followed. The first priority then was to increase the number of grammar school places. Since 1946 eleven new grammar technical schools were built, and the five existing ones were enlarged. Forty-three new secondary modern schools were also built, many of them with G.C.E. streams, so that by the early sixties more than 30 per cent of the pupils in a year group were given the opportunity to take a course leading to G.C.E. The cost of this expansion had been of the order of nearly eleven million pounds. In the meantime, the education committee had kept a careful eye on comprehensive developments elsewhere, and even tried a few canny experiments of its own. In 1956 it ran the rule over the comprehensive schools then in existence in London, Coventry, and West Bromwich, deciding that it would be another ten years before any decision could be reached on the effectiveness of

57

the system, and that in any case large comprehensive schools would not be suitable for many areas in County Durham. But nevertheless, they tried their hand at a small one. They felt that upper Weardale was a closely knit, long-established community with sound traditions, and that here, if anywhere in the county, the comprehensive idea had a good chance of success. So they extended Wolsingham Grammar School— a small seventeenth-century school—by adding modern buildings and amenities at a short distance from the old school— thus creating Wolsingham Secondary School to cater for all types of secondary education in a comprehensive fashion in upper Weardale. An experiment of a different kind was tried in the rapidly growing town of Billingham. A large plant provided a rapidly growing population, as yet without community spirit or local roots, a complete contrast to Weardale. As a large site was available, it was decided to build one grammar technical school with up to four associated secondary modern schools on the same campus, each with its own headmaster, class-room block, assembly hall and dining-rooms, but sharing such facilities as science laboratories, housecraft rooms, workshops and gymnasia. By grouping the schools together it was possible to provide a swimming bath and a sports hall. All pupils were to wear the same blazers and caps, with only a badge to differentiate between the schools or 'halls'. It was hoped that these arrangements would make it easier to transfer pupils from one 'hall' to another when the need arose without arousing emotional problems or complications. In 1962 the education committee tried yet a third experiment, in some ways a development from the idea of the Billingham Campus. This was to set up multilateral units. Each multilateral unit would consist of one existing grammar technical school and a number of neighbouring secondary modern schools. There would be one board of governors to control all the schools in the unit. There would be frequent meetings of heads to co-ordinate developments, and there were to be similar courses in the basic subjects in the first two years, to ease transfer from one school to the other if it seemed desirable. It was expected that each secondary modern school in the multilateral unit would develop some speciality of its own to give it standing in the eyes of its pupils and the public. This might be a technical bias, a commercial course, special attention to speech or drama, or anything else which might suggest itself. The experiment was greatly helped by the abolition in 1963-4 of the selection examination for grammar school places, and its replacement by a scheme for the guidance of children into the type of secondary course best suited for them, based on their primary school reports. Great stress was laid on the fact that these placings were provisional only, and that if they proved to be wrong later, adjustments and transfers would be made by a committee composed of the heads of the multilateral unit concerned. This was an interesting approach towards fluidity and ease of transfer, a flexible type of secondary education on comprehensive lines, though not in distinctive comprehensive schools. Now that it is coming to be realized that it does not appear to be essential that all comprehensive schools have to be mammoths of 2,400 pupils, it has been agreed that there is a place in Durham County for eight form or twelve form entry comprehensive schools. So in areas where there has been no new building, and in new towns such as Washington, the decision has been made to build comprehensive schools. But it will give you some idea of the time scheme when I tell you that it has been estimated that at the present rate of building it will take at least forty years to complete reorganization into comprehensive schools, and it may well be that before this time has elapsed an entirely new form of secondary education has superseded the comprehensives. The present problem, of course, is how to proceed without making redundant the expensive post-war schools already built.

With all this as background, let us study the reorganization negotiations on which I wish to concentrate in considerable detail. Our Director of Education had ruled for many years, with great energy, some panache, and immense determination. Rather autocratic, as he probably needed to be, he had since the war devoted his energies to building fine secondary modern schools of which any city might be proud. Certainly, as he neared retirement in 1964, it was true to say that the physical conditions of the secondary modern schools were far superior to those of the grammar schools, and that these new schools were beginning to show a distinctive life and personality of their own. G.C.E. courses had been started there, and continuation courses linked them with the fine new technical college. There was, in fact, provision for something like 40 per cent of the children in any year group in the city to take a G.C.E. course, either in a grammar school or a secondary modern school, and transfer to the sixth form of a grammar school, or to the advanced studies at the technical college, was easy and informal. This development had been expedited by the overwhelming Labour majority on the City Council. The more doctrinaire members of this majority had been anxious for some time to 'abolish the 11 +', and when it came to appointing a successor to the retiring director they were clearly determined to appoint a man who, amongst other things, was prepared to press on with educational reorganization as quickly as possible. So it proved, and within days of taking up his post the new Director issued to the Development and Planning Sub-Committee his first Report on Secondary Reorganization.

It was an unexceptionable document, such as one might have hoped to get from any sensible public servant faced with the task of carrying out a lightning reorganization of a complex system of schools, most of which he had not seen, and none of which he knew in detail. It appeared to open the flood-gates, and in one sense it did, since it tacitly assumed that there could be no question of leaving things as they were; but it was really a matter of playing for time. It started off by underlining the special local difficulties. The City boundaries were about to be revised, and no one knew what additions to the City area this would bring. The existing grammar schools were unusually successful and well-established institutions, of such great prestige locally (and in one case nationally) that many people would be upset to see them disturbed; and, ironically enough, the nature and disposition of the existing secondary modern schools, entirely due to the forward looking policies of the education committee and the energy of the previous Director, were now a complicating issue. They were palatial institutions, built in lovely playing fields, and though ideally placed for their present tasks were set in the wrong parts of the city if they were to become entirely neighbourhood schools. Any scheme of reorganization, it warned the committee, must be based on the fullest possible knowledge of the facts, both concerning the size and disposition of future age groups, and concerning the best use of the existing buildings; it must be an improvement on the existing system, which implied the retention of the highest possible educational standards for children of great ability equally with the improvement of opportunity for children at other ability levels; it must be fully discussed with those who would be required to operate it; it must be fully explained to the parents of the city; and it must be based on a clear philosophy. What was the reason for wanting change, the Committee was urged to ask itself, and what, after all, the purpose of secondary education? There are great differences of ability, and these differences need nurturing by different educational techniques; did the Committee wish this different treatment to be given in separate institutions or in single institutions? Did the Committee wish children to attend area schools, and did they want a uniform pattern for the entire City? In any case, the Development Plan for primary and secondary education, drawn up after the 1944 Act, was now twenty years old and would need extensive revision. In the meantime, there were six possible alternative schemes for reorganization, which the Report then described in bare outline. A seventh possibility, a complete set of new all-in comprehensive schools dealing with all children from the age of 11 to 18, which the Committee really favoured, was dismissed as a 'non-starter' because of the expense involved. This was a far cry from the hustings, where slogans about 'dishing the grammar schools' and 'abolishing the 11 +' could always be relied on to pick up a few votes. The questions were fundamental: 'why', 'when', and above all 'how'. Clearly the Committee was in for a spot of hard thinking—though I do not think any of them had any idea of quite how long and how hard it was going to be.

Now Directors of Education who write such Reports are also animals who laugh and weep. To the outside world they are the great panjandrums who know all that there is to be known about schools, and teachers, and education of all kinds from the cradle to the grave—and to be perfectly fair, one meets the odd one who starts to measure up to this impossible requirement; one meets more who can talk persuasively, and have an enviable facility for giving the impression that they do come somewhere near it. Teachers in their area expect them to be commanding personalities, always right and full of infinite understanding, professional colleagues of a superior kind with the gift of leadership, twentieth-century Moses who will show them how to reach the promised land. But teachers are also an irreverent band of individualists, capable of telling even Moses what to do with his tablets of stone. There is a deep tradition amongst them that the class-room is the real battle-field where active service is to be found, and an even deeper distrust of those sitting in City Hall. To the councillors, the Director is their chief executive, whose principal task is to find out what they want done, and then go away and do it. They are the masters, he is the servant. But he has tactfully to help them make up their collective mind, steering them away from what he knows to be mistakes, or pushing them gently in the direction of what he hopes is right, or if not right at least expedient. There are times when the servant has to be the master, and he has to decide the policy as well as carry it out. He must be a born manipulator of committees or he is lost, and this calls for a strange mixture of high principle and low cunning—the qualities of a Delphic Oracle and a brooding Buddha combined. Behind the façade, of course, they are puzzled, worried little men like the rest of us, only anxious to do the best they can with a fearful problem for which there is no rapid solution.

The Committee, too, for whom these Reports are written, is equally anxious to do the best it can, whatever political favours the members may happen to be wearing at the time. I would not impute unworthy motives to any of them, nor give either side the monopoly of wisdom and understanding. I would say, however, that they are all, for better or for worse, firmly in the grip of the political game as it is played in this country, and thoroughly enjoy playing it. It has a tang and flavour all its own. Once you have tasted this heady draught you rapidly become addicted. It is well worth long hours in dim dusty committee rooms, and a certain amount of public vilification. The first rule of the game is that if you are a member of the loyal opposition you will find yourself playing up the slope into the teeth of a howling gale, with everything against you. You may persuade yourself that you are having influence and getting somewhere, but the harsh reality is that in important matters you are well-nigh powerless. If you are a member of the majority party you are easily persuaded of your own importance, and can achieve a good deal more, but you rapidly become aware of the second important rule. There is a small, imprecisely defined, group of more able and more senior or influential councillors, who set the pace and make the real decisions. This is the caucus. Inside the caucus, exerting more influence still, are two men—the group leader and his heir apparent. These two form the real nucleus of power. As long as they retain the respect and confidence of the caucus, forming close ranks around them like some Praetorian guard, and do not lose complete touch with the larger body of ordinary council members, they wield remarkable power, and enjoy a position of such independence that it is they who provide the motive power and urgency without which the whole ramshackle system of local government by committee would fall apart. It is this nucleus which the Director must in the last resort direct, and control, and serve; and it is this Praetorian guard which the working headmaster has somehow to penetrate and influence if his advice is to be anything more than empty wind.

Now the Director's first Report was such an unexceptionable document that, if the Committee had taken its pious platitudes seriously, they would have been all the way towards accepting my ten guarantees before the controversy even started. It could have been published in every newspaper, or stuck on every billboard for everyone to read; indeed, it would have been a great public service if it had been. Instead, it was marked 'Highly Confidential', and given severely restricted circulation. There was a perfectly good technical reason for this. It was a Report to a private sub-committee, which could only report to the main committee which had set it up, and it would have been an offence against the conventions of committee-dom for it to make its deliberations public. The leaky colander of City Hall security made it certain that everyone knew that something was afoot, and many were the tales of axes being sharpened and blows about to fall. Copies were issued to the teachers' associations in the city and the Direct Grant schools, and their observations were called for inside three weeks. These were the last three weeks of the summer term, which are busy and exhausting weeks at the best of times. It was just not physically possible in the time to consult the bulk of teachers, but the executive committees of the various associations ran themselves into the earth, and a separate document went in from each association on time. They appeared to be self-contradictory, although as we shall see a good deal of this was apparent rather than real; but they were all agreed in asking for more time to consider the implications, more opportunities for discussion, and more details of what each of the six schemes outlined meant in local terms. Some of us felt it had been a tactical error to make such important statements in such a rushed way, and that it would be a strategic disaster if the teachers could not some how contrive to speak with one voice instead of five.

Weeks passed until at the end of October 1964 the sub-committee received a second Director's Report. This provided them with heavy schedules of facts and figures, giving them the estimated size of future age groups, and the accommodation available in existing secondary schools. It examined in slightly more detail the six possible types of reorganization mentioned in the first Report, giving some indication of the viability of each in the light of the local statistics which had just been presented to them. It also drew the attention of the sub-committee to what the five teachers' associations had had to say. Suggestions made by two of these associations, that a series of professional visits might be made to evaluate experiments already made in other areas, and public lectures should be arranged to allow knowledgeable outsiders to make their experience available, were seen to be sensible, and arrangements were made for these to happen over the next few months. The Committee also, at this point, started to dig its heels in and show its independence. These six schemes were all very well, it said, but what about the seventh which had been dismissed so early from the field as a 'non-starter'? They wanted the Director to give them next time a more detailed account of how a complete set of all-through, $11 +$ to $18+$, comprehensives could be introduced to the city—because that was what the more doctrinaire members really wanted. They also showed active interest in the sixth scheme, possibly because there was a wholesome root and branch aura about it, and also because it had all the attractions of forbidden fruit.

There had been a fairly recent amendment to the Education

Act permitting the ages of transfer from infant to junior and from junior to secondary schools to be changed from 7+ and 11+ respectively. The West Riding had used this opportunity to carry out an experiment in a limited area—indeed, it is probably true to say that it was their determination to do so which brought about the change in the law. Why should the committee not decide to 'do a West Riding', and set up a completely new pattern of primary schools for children from five to nine, intermediate schools for children from nine to thirteen, with secondary schools (non-selective of course) for those beyond thirteen? The short answer was that the Minister would not accept it. Educationally, there was everything to be said for a complete rethink of all stages of school life, and if one was really serious about social justice and equality of opportunity one would start with a nation-wide system of nursery schools, and an interdepartmental blitz by all the welfare services on the interrelated problems of the slums (rural as well as urban) and the twilight areas. The official mind boggled at the predicament it would be in if it woke up all these slumbering dogs at once. It took refuge behind the fact that the Plowden Report was considering the age of transfer, and it said it could do nothing until it had reported. In the meantime, there were to be no more 'West Ridings'. But the Director was instructed to make a direct approach to Whitehall to see if we could be treated as a special case. By the 24th of November he was able to tell them that permission would not be given. 11+ as the age of transfer was sacrosanct and immovable. With all the wisdom of hindsight it is possible to see what an atrociously bad decision this was. Firing squads are a little out of fashion, but one is tempted to think that the well-meaning gentlemen who made this decision might in all justice be asked to face one. They condemned us all to many months of tedious and completely fruitless negotiation. Without knowing it, they had taken the decision right out of local hands, and made it practically certain that the city was to be saddled with a two-tier system of secondary schools which would have been educationally and socially indefensible. I say 'practically' certain, because it was only by the grace of God, and at times by the helpful nudges of a whole series of benevolent devils, that this fate was avoided.

To do them justice, the men from Whitehall did try to be helpful by saying that the Secretary of State would be issuing a directive on the reorganization of secondary education in the near future. It seemed reasonable to expect that this would make all things plain, and only sensible to wait to see what it said before rushing into action. The weeks passed and on January 21st 1965 there was a debate in the House when the Government made their intentions abundantly plain, but still no directive explaining how it was to be done appeared. There was therefore understandable impatience amongst the local politicians to get on with it and do something when the Director reported to the sub-committee for the third time in April of 1965. There was a subtle change of mood in the Report to take account of this impatience. Though it was still impeccably fair on the surface, presenting points for and points against in a quite disarming way, it was arguing now instead of just explaining, and presented the Committee with a ready-made solution to their problem, if they cared to take it. After all, that is what chief executives are for.

The six or seven possible schemes were now narrowed down to three; and by the end of this Report the three little nigger boys had been whittled down to one.

First it dealt with all-through comprehensives from 11+ to 18+. Clearly, from the 'administrative' point of view, this troublesome 'non-starter', which persisted in getting up and trotting gaily round the course, had to be shot with a humane killer. For the purposes of that meeting, it was! Yes, it had attractions. It abolished external selection, and got rid of segregation based on intellectual ability. Easy transfer within the school from stream to stream and course to course would be possible. Large schools like these could offer a wide variety of courses, and so on. But locally, there were eight powerful disadvantages. They had all been mentioned by the teachers in their hurried observations nine or ten months ago, but it was pleasant to see our heresies of yester-year reappearing as part of holy writ. As these would be by nature area schools, there was a great danger of selection by social background replacing selection by ability. To have adequate sixth forms and to be otherwise effective, they would need to be very large, with resulting problems of control and organization. They really

66

needed to be housed in purpose-built accommodation as 'a so-called comprehensive school, comprising separate and distant buildings, is a travesty of an educational institution'. It was questionable whether for the next twenty years there would be enough academically well-qualified specialist teachers for the abler pupils if they were spread over such a system of schools. Headmasters of rare ability would be required to give the necessary leadership to such schools, and they were in even shorter supply. To concentrate the available building resources on these vast emporia would starve developments in other fields of education. It would be dangerous to allow comprehensive and traditional grammar schools to exist side by side; either children in the catchment area must be prevented from going to grammar schools with a consequent outcry by many parents (who have votes in local elections), or the schools must face up to losing most of the top ability range and so not be truly comprehensive. Finally, though they could be introduced locally in four clearly defined phases, and though the first phase would as it happens be relatively easy, phases two, three, and four would be bound to extend over a period of twenty or thirty years. This last point clinched it. One little nigger boy sank without trace, at least for the time being; for the ironic fact was that he was needed at a later stage, and it took a great deal of effort to fish him up from the depths and pump a little wind into his poor little lungs.

But meantime there was scheme number two which needed attention. This called for the conversion of all the secondary modern schools and some of the grammar schools into junior comprehensive schools, with pupils from eleven to sixteen, with advanced work after that age concentrated in one sixth form college. The advantages and disadvantages of this idea were faithfully set out. There was just a chance that this could start to operate in September 1967, though there were two major difficulties. There would have to be additional building of laboratories and other specialist accommodation at quite a number of schools, and the specialist staffs at the existing grammar schools would have to be redeployed. There was another minor detail. The well-established boys' grammar school—with its distinguished academic record and its unrivalled local esteem—would have to be the Sixth Form College. Now it is a curious fact in provincial cities that such an outstandingly successful school attracts to itself a powerful love-hate relationship. It arouses deep affection and profound respect in the minds of some, extracts lip service rather grudgingly from many more, and must always be aware that just around the corner is an army of 'knockers', anxious to take it down a peg or two, and make it get back into line. To raise it on to a lonely pedestal and call it 'College', and to make all the other secondary schools subordinate and contributory to it, was to take the exact opposite course to that which a number of 'egalitarian' minds had intended. Local prejudice alone made this little nigger boy a hopeless contender.

And then there was one. The third scheme was for all children to transfer at the age of 11 to Junior High Schools, developed from the existing secondary modern schools, where they would stay for a period of three years. Then they would all transfer to Upper Schools, developed from the existing grammar schools, where they would complete their secondary education. Apart from certain additions to the existing grammar schools, it would also be necessary to build one completely new Upper School of 1,000 places, a site for which had been provisionally ear-marked within the last few weeks. Apart from these considerations, 'this plan is the one to which existing buildings could be most easily adapted', and it 'could probably be introduced in 1967'. The Report came right out into the open in its final paragraph.

It may be that the Sub-Committee are of the opinion, in the light of the foregoing, that Scheme III (a Two-Tier System), is the only one that has sufficiently few serious disadvantages, and is reasonably capable of institution in the foreseeable future. If so, the Sub-Committee may wish me to prepare a detailed scheme on these lines for consideration by the Sub-Committee at a later date, and then for consideration by other interested parties.

The sub-committee were of this opinion!

This was careful diplomatic language, but it could not disguise that a fundamental decision had been made. It had been made too, on barefaced grounds of administrative convenience, speed, and cheapness, and educational interests, particularly the teachers and the parents were not to be consulted until it was too cut and dried to do much about it. After very nearly a year of considering various possibilities the local politicians felt it was high time they settled for some scheme or other—any scheme—even one for which the best that could be said was that it 'has sufficiently few serious disadvantages'. What a clarion call that was with which to storm the barricades! Still, they expected to have only a few lonely voices raised against them, and with the usual mixture of bluster and half truth they felt pretty confident that they could win over 'the other interested parties'. Certainly, the rest of the City felt that a definite scheme had finally been worked out. Almost before the sub-committee had finished its private deliberations, the local press announced in banner headlines what the new educational structure in the City was going to be. How it got its scoop has never been satisfactorily explained, and it was no part of the sub-committee's plan that the news should be broken in this way. But it was, and it did great harm, coming as a particularly nasty jolt to the teachers of the City, who felt justifiably annoyed that their first intimation of a decision which affected them so closely should come through the letter-box with the evening paper. They were quick to see that it meant the 'beheading' of every secondary modern school in the City and the loss of their senior pupils to the grammar schools, which in a fine fit of sub-editorial frenzy were dubbed in the headlines, not Upper Schools, but 'Super Schools'. As flustered and worried parents began ringing up and calling to find out what all this meant in terms of their little Willy, teachers had to admit that they did not know. A series of articles written later in the local press gave the Director a chance to explain in more sober detail what was in fact intended, and meetings were arranged to allow parents to find out more about it, but the damage was already done. It seems incredible that the city fathers should be so hopelessly inept at their public relations. The campaign of explanation, when it did come, left everyone concerned with a strong feeling that the die was irrevocably cast—that we now had a scheme—that this, in other words, was it!

Grin and bear it, and try to work it, was the most constructive advice one could find at this point; but much more than this was required of any working headmaster with the best interests of his school at heart. He could publicly condemn the scheme, and set himself up in open opposition to his employers, taking up the familiar line of 'over my dead body'. Many in other parts of the country did this; it was a great relief to the feelings; but a brief halo of martyrdom was a poor exchange for complete loss of influence as the juggernaut moved on, and move on it always did. This policy of despair was therefore rejected. It seemed better to accept the unpalatable fact that Local Authority Schools do not belong to the staff who work in them, or even to the section of parents whose children happen to be pupils in a particular school, but to the Local Authority; and after due process, that Local Authority is perfectly entitled to do exactly what it wants with them. Moreover, at that point it is entitled to demand that all teachers in its schools will strain every nerve to make its scheme work—'grin and bear it, and try to work it'—or else leave its employ. But whatever the politicians, the city, and the bulk of the teachers seemed to think, we had not reached that point yet. Between a 'declaration of intent' and the implementation of a scheme was a period of time which could and should be profitably used. This was no time for timid yes-men. Teacher opinion must be mobilized to bring forcibly to the attention of the committee the grave educational weaknesses of the scheme it now proposed. But how?

First of all, it was necessary to give teacher opinion a chance to formulate itself. I sat down with my professional colleagues in my own school to work out in some detail what we thought the effect of the scheme would be on the school we knew best. Then, without associating the staff in any way with what I intended to say, I made a personal statement to the governors of my school. I told them frankly of the staff enquiry, and said that when it was completed it would be brought to their notice. Meanwhile they should know that their Headmaster intended to do all that he could to expose the weaknesses of the proposed scheme. As the days slipped past, it became clear that ours was not the only school to feel concern, and as the various and separate associations of teachers met, that there was growing dissatisfaction amongst teachers with what the Committee proposed, but as yet this was confused and uncoordinated.

It was at this point that an unexpected catalyst was

accidentally introduced. It first appeared in the secondary modern schools. Two or three thoughtful schoolmasters in one of these schools, horrified at the impact that the proposed scheme was likely to have on their own school, came across a full copy of the working papers for a scheme which was to be applied in Doncaster. This started by accepting the obvious fact that full 'comprehension' was not possible for twenty or thirty years, and that in the meantime two things were essential. One was to bind together the secondary modern schools and the grammar schools into a comprehensive cocoon from which they could not escape; the other was to see that they retained sufficient independence to continue doing what each was best suited to doing until they could be united in one big purpose-built comprehensive school. At the age of 11, all children of all ranges of ability were to enter the secondary modern schools, and stay there for two years. Then, if a parent wished his child to stay in full-time schooling until the age of 18+, he could ask for the child to transfer to a grammar school. If a parent thought it more likely that his child would wish to leave school at 15 or 16, he could choose to keep him in the secondary modern school. Each secondary modern school would run courses for the 'O' Level G.C.E. and the C.S.E., and any child who had done well enough at 16 to merit further study could do this by joining either a grammar school sixth form, or the appropriate course in the technical college. This completely removed the sting of 11 + selection, since the senior members of the secondary modern schools were there—not because they had 'failed'—but because they had chosen to stay. It also offered real parental choice—with professional advice available for those who needed it. It brought about considerable widening in the ability range of both secondary modern and grammar schools, without making this too great to be accommodated in the existing buildings. If it was true that the only possible scheme for us was a Two-Tier Scheme, here was an alternative way of introducing a dynamic and sophisticated system, as opposed to our static and clumsy plan of 'All change' at the calendar age of 14. Moreover, it had been introduced by an even more solidly Labour Council than our own, and accepted by a Labour Minister of Education as being a workmanlike interim scheme.

Could this be the answer to our predicament? As copies of the Doncaster Plan were passed from hand to hand, a growing number of teachers became sure it was worth further investigation. It seemed to us that the sub-committee had been insufficiently briefed on this possibility, if indeed they had ever heard of it—and the rather undignified scurry to get copies for them one weekend inclines me to the latter view. Parents, too, as they came to hear of it, began to express great interest. After all, some choice in their children's school was what they really wanted, and this seemed a possible way to get it. Pardonable irritation began to appear amongst the official Town Hall spokesmen. After all, when you are trying to rivet public attention on the rather dreary one-horse race you happen to be running, it is tiresome to see a completely unofficial but far more glamorous entrant trying to come under starter's orders. But I must not mislead you. It never did start. Perhaps it never could have started. Its real importance was that it provided teachers with a talking point—a ray of hope at their darkest hour—a proof that members of all teaching associations, the staffs of all types of schools, could meet together on common ground and make their presence felt.

It led directly to the calling of a strictly private and unofficial meeting of the President and the Secretary of the local Head Teachers' Association, the National Union of Teachers, the National Association of Schoolmasters, and the Joint Four Secondary Associations. It was unanimously decided that a joint letter, signed by everybody present, should be released for publication. This appeared in the local press on the 22nd of June 1965. It was remarkable for two things; for what it did not say, and for the impressive list of people who were so obviously at one in not saying it. It said we had been examining the proposed scheme, which everybody knew; and would make our views known through the proper channels in due course, which I imagine everybody expected. But it added the one cryptic paragraph: 'Whilst welcoming changes which can be shown to constitute real and genuine educational progress, they have misgivings about certain aspects of the scheme as it has been outlined.' But it didn't say what these 'misgivings' were. This was deliberate and intentional. It was the old teaching trick of the rhetorical pause—by saying nothing at all for several pained seconds you reduce the noisy and unruly class to silence as they begin to wonder what on earth it can be that you aren't saying. The Press jumped in with a rousing editorial entitled, 'The Vital Voice', which sums up the situation better than I can.

It has been said that when two or three teachers are gathered together a dispute arises. This may be a little unjust, but it is no secret that there are usually quite sharp differences of opinion between the various teaching bodies. The more significant then is the brief letter which heads our correspondence columns today—significant because it represents the rare event of four quite separate teaching organizations in the city standing united. At least the letter can be taken as an earnest that the teachers are giving great thought as one body to the problems inherent in the introduction of any comprehensive system. More important is the indication that in acknowledging that they have an important part to play in shaping the great changes which we feel must come, they are anxious to do this in the correct way and at the right time. But is the course they are set upon the right one? We do not think so. We have heard the politicians on comprehensive education, we have heard the administrators, and we have heard from the public. Only one vital voice is missing. It is surely right that we should hear also from the men and women best qualified of all to know what may be right for the girls and boys they teach. For it must never for one moment be overlooked that these new proposals, although they may in the event bring administrative and other side advantages, have the education of the children as their sole reason for existence. Today's letter speaks of misgivings about certain aspects of the scheme. Obviously the teachers have something important to say. They are offering their advice through their consultative body in private. The parents and the public, we feel, should know what that advice is, and they should know now, because vital proposals are being framed now.

The Press was nearer the mark than it knew. Wherever two teachers are gathered together there are three opinions. Our delightful habit of splitting hairs and chopping logic at public meetings had so deafened the public that they could not hear what we were all trying to say. What it called our 'consultative body in private' was in even worse shape. The new Director had tried to set up new consultative machinery. There was to be a Joint Consultative Committee, one half composed of the leading elected members of the Education Committee, the other a Teachers' Panel representing the various teachers' organizations. The Joint Consultative Committee had never met. The Teachers' Panel had met regularly every month in City Hall, but to remarkably little effect. It was ignored, since political realists were mindful of the notorious divisions in the teaching profession, and did not seriously consider consulting it. It was precisely because it was determined to end or mend this deplorable state of affairs that the self-appointed teachers' caucus had rushed into print. 'What are your "misgivings"?' demanded further editorials, and an expectant public listened carefully for the Vital Voice. It was silent, and the teaching profession of the city was in a difficult position. Who could possibly speak for it? The Teachers' Panel of the Joint Consultative Committee, said the unofficial caucus, passing the hot potato rapidly along the line, and establishing at one move its own legitimacy, and its own Praetorian guard. Certainly, said the Teachers' Panel, heavily impregnated with caucus members, and we will appoint a Working Party to draw up our Joint Statement, passing the job rapidly back to the key members of the caucus, our own nucleus of power. You see, we had learnt a lot in the last twelve months about the rules of the political game. We had even got a certain sense of elation from the witty timing of our original *démarche*. The 'misgivings' letter had coincided exactly with the final one of a series of official articles which had been designed to conclude the matter as far as the public was concerned; and the effect of our letter was to reopen it by introducing a piece of glorious uncertainty. 'We will speak in our own good time', thundered a holding letter from the Teachers' Panel, as we desperately settled down to work out what we were going to say.

But this time we worked from the top downwards, rather than the other way round. The first stage was simple. We had a member of each association bring the original 'observations' of his association to an informal meeting, and pass it round for the others to read. Never mind the points with which you disagree, the instruction went, just put a tick against any point you notice in another association's document with which you are certain your own association would agree. In five minutes each document was covered with ticks, indicating what some of us suspected all along, that there were wide grounds of agreement between all the teaching associations. A drafting committee then set to work to draw up a document which faithfully expressed this wide general agreement, with special reference to this proposed scheme. It was passed down to associations for comment, and back up to the Teachers' Panel for final approval. It was accepted by them with complete unanimity on July 21st 1965, without it being necessary to change so much as a comma. The drafting committee had got right to the heart of the matter, and brought out the basic agreement which had existed amongst teachers all the time without even the teachers themselves being aware of it. It was not a moment too soon, since the next day there was to be a crucial meeting of the sub-committee, when we suspected vital decisions were about to be made. The vital voice had to speak now, or for ever remain silent.

Eight or nine days before this, by the way, another voice had spoken. The Department of Education and Science issued Circular 10/65, its long-awaited directive. It was a curiously strangulated, uncertain, not to say self-contradictory, almost shabby performance—which must have caused great dismay to those who had been expecting so much from it. Instead of the firm, rock-like foundation for a major social reform, it displayed for all to see the shifting quicksands on which we were being asked to build. It made absolutely certain that, in five or ten years from now, a major Education Act will have to be rushed through the Commons, to introduce some rhyme and reason into the tremendously complicated lack of pattern which will by that time have emerged in the field of secondary education. Over the top into action you must go, it told the Local Authorities, and the best of British luck; but mind you don't get your feet wet, and please remember we can't provide the ammunition and reinforcements which we know you are going to need. Twelve months from today you must let us have your final plans, showing in complete detail what you propose to do in the next three years, and in fair detail your long-term proposals. There are six main forms of comprehensive organization you may choose, some of which we like, and some of which we don't like but are prepared to tolerate. You may work out your own local variant of any one or more of these; indeed, if your area is large enough and you think that local circumstances warrant it, you may conceivably have all six schemes working in different parts of it. But if you are attracted to scheme five (Sixth Form Colleges), for heaven's sake come and talk to us about it before you commit yourselves, since so very little is definitely known about them, that by pooling our common lack of knowledge we may be mutually enlightened. Be particularly wary of scheme six—which depends on altering the 11 + age of transfer and the creation of middle schools on the West Riding pattern. We find this very attractive indeed— and you will probably find it so too; but we haven't the slightest intention of agreeing to the general introduction of such schemes. We are as conscious as you are that the character and size of the existing buildings must condition to an important degree the education that is given in them. But—

during the next few years growing demands for new schools arising from the increase in the school population, new house building and the raising of the school leaving age are unlikely to permit any re-laxation of the criteria for inclusion of projects in building program-mes. It would not be realistic for authorities to plan on the basis that their individual programmes will be increased solely to take account of the need to adapt or remodel existing buildings on a scale which would not have been necessary but for reorganization.

Moreover, there will be no extra teachers available, since, 'the Secretary of State will not be able to modify the quota arrangements to take account of individual authorities' proposals in response to this Circular'. In fact, this Circular told our hard-headed councillors nothing that they did not know already about the complicated and difficult task on which they were engaged; but it did emphasize the impossible nature of the tasks they were being called upon to perform. It was now that every Local Authority in the country, of all political persuasions, should have spoken with one voice. Enough of this mealy-mouthed hypocrisy, they should have said. If you will the ends, you must will the means, and until you do it is a complete nonsense to expect us to work out satisfactory schemes. But they did not. It was at this point, in my view, that the existing Local Authorities and their principal officers laid down and

died, and I for one will shed no tears when most of them disappear in the complete overhaul of local government which is
shortly to be introduced.

Certainly our sub-committee was in a considerably chast-
ened, not to say disgruntled, mood when it met on July 22nd.
They were given a painfully one-sided briefing on the mys-
terious Doncaster Plan, which seemed to be a popular topic
of conversation amongst everybody except themselves. They
heard that snags had arisen in their own pet scheme, and
it would have to be delayed from 1967 until 1968 at the
earliest. They were presented with further details of it, and
were called upon to make a whole series of difficult and
involved decisions. With such a long and tiring agenda, it
would have been expecting too much of human nature to
think that they would welcome yet one more piece of paper—
*An Interim Statement of the Teachers' Panel of the Joint Advisory
Committee*. They galloped through it with perfunctory, almost
insulting, rapidity, and when our teacher representative
attempted to speak to it, he was met with unconcealed hostility.
This was a great mistake. It showed the teachers that whatever
its public protestations might be, the sub-committee was not
at this time prepared to listen to what the teachers were
trying to say.

But had not the press and public been demanding to hear
what the teachers had to say? This was the time to tell them,
loudly and clearly. It was time to give the sub-committee and
the Director an object lesson in how to handle public relations.
There was an immediate press hand-out of our 'Interim Statement', and in preparation for just this necessity its length and
phraseology had been carefully calculated to have the maximum
effect on the largest possible audience. It was splashed with
banner headlines over the local papers, with editorial comment
and T.V. coverage for good measure. We stressed that we
were quite unanimous in all our findings. We said we were
justifiably proud of the achievements of the schools of all types
in the city in which our members served, seeing them as
institutions which had made an important contribution to the
education of children of all classes; yet we were well aware
that they still fell short of providing the complete educational
umbrella which the city so obviously needed for the future.

If the abolition of the 11+, and the end of the system of segregating children at 11 in separate schools on this basis alone were necessary preliminaries to this desirable progress—and we conceded that the majority of our teachers thought they were—then we saw little point in clamouring for their retention. So as far as this went we welcomed the declared aims of the Education Committee, since they were our aims too. But we stressed that in any system which supplanted the present one, there would still be a necessity for certain kinds of selection in certain circumstances. Objective diagnostic tests would still be necessary, for instance, to determine a child's suitability for the courses it wished to take; and in our view it was also important for the parents to be given some real say in determining the course which the child should follow.

We then turned to examine some of the broader principles involved in their scheme—which proposed that children would all spend the first three years of their secondary education in a Junior High School with a local catchment area, and at the age of 14 would all transfer to one of four Senior High Schools, each with a slightly different educational bias, and each drawing its pupils from the city as a whole, and not from any defined area—promising, or threatening, to go into more detail at some later stage. Firstly, we said that for this system to work smoothly it would be necessary to coordinate the curriculum, the syllabus, and the teaching methods of all Junior and Senior High Schools in the city in a very detailed way, since any child might end up at any Senior High. This would have the unfortunate effect of removing from the Junior High Schools the freedom to develop their individual school personalities. They would be schools with no definite purpose of their own, except to act as feeder schools for the Senior High Schools, and should this happen it would be difficult to recruit suitable staff for them, since all teachers prefer to work in schools which have a separate life and character of their own. Secondly, we said that we were unanimously of the opinion that automatic transfer of all at 14 years of age, as proposed, was not sound educational practice. In the case of children who were going forward to take their G.C.E. or C.S.E., it would leave them only four to five effective terms in the Senior High School in which to settle in and complete their course. In the case of the lower ability groups, transfer at 14 would pose even more difficult problems. The existing secondary modern schools had now acquired the courses, techniques, activities and teaching staff to give these children suitable instruction of a practical nature. But with reorganization the courses and specialist staffs of these schools would be split up. The continuity would be gone. The Senior High Schools would constitute a separate two-year school life for these children, and unless a tremendous amount of new building and equipment was provided to give them practical courses in their fresh schools, they would be worse off educationally than they were at present. Here we threw in for good measure what Circular 10/65 had to say about two-tier systems with a transfer age of 14:

Pupils would enter the senior school at a stage when the number of subjects studied was being reduced and the course began to focus more narrowly on examinations. Some subjects would never be begun, either because they needed a course of some years or because they were not subjects which the particular pupil needed to offer in an examination. Although for subjects such as history and geography the age chosen for transfer might not be very important, for others, such as science and modern languages, delay of transfer until 14 would probably be harmful. A two-year course geared to an external examination would be likely to be planned on the basis of giving a large amount of time to comparatively few subjects; this is the very reverse of liberal education.

Thirdly, we reminded them that it had just been stated that there would be no extra money available for reorganization as such in the immediate future, and though this problem was theirs rather than ours, it looked as though their scheme needed considerable expenditure, or it would have to be introduced in such a makeshift manner that it would not be successful. Fourthly, we knew there was to be no increase in the number of teachers available, and this we felt would seriously limit what we were able to achieve in the near future. We pointed out that Circular 10/65 called for 'progress to be as rapid as possible' but it was not to be achieved 'by the adoption of plans whose educational disadvantages more than offset the benefits which will flow from the adoption of Comprehensive schooling'. This we felt might well happen if they implemented their present scheme. We therefore suggested that before it was finally adopted they should carry out a full professional investigation into the merits of two-tier systems already introduced, not excluding the Doncaster Plan.

There was an immediate explosion of bad temper, taking the form of a long rambling official letter to the press, attacking Doncaster and all its works, and by implication cracking the whip to call this unruly bunch of teachers to heel. Never mind Doncaster, came the icy riposte from the Teachers' Panel, that is only mentioned in passing in one short sentence right at the end; concentrate on answering the charges in the main body of our Interim Statement, for on those your scheme will stand or fall. Rapidly the anger disappeared, largely because the blustering threats had not the slightest effect on the teachers, but were causing adverse comment amongst the public at large. An offer was made that certain leading members of the sub-committee would graciously condescend to listen to what the teachers had to say. This was indignantly refused by the teachers, who made a counter-proposition. A promise was then extorted that as early as possible in the next term the Joint Consultative Committee—elected representatives as well as teachers—would meet for the first time. Joint consultation was about to begin.

This vital meeting took place on September 29th 1965. Teacher caucus and council caucus had now met face to face, and one working headmaster at least was delighted to see that what he had at one time despaired of had at long last happened. But what would be the outcome? The teachers were aware of the danger of it turning into a slanging match. They had therefore appointed a single spokesman to express their views, limiting their own interventions to emphasizing the general point he had just made, or bringing in additional details which would support it. This enabled a powerful case to be put with the maximum power—aided immeasurably, it is right to say, by the meticulous fairness of the senior alderman in the chair. A valuable exchange of views took place, and it began to become clear to the councillors that the glib official answers of the Director to our 'misgivings' were not real answers at all.

Working within the general pattern the Teachers' Panel had by this time laid down, the staff of individual schools now began to take a hand. One girls' school invited the sub-committee to coffee, and showed them on the ground what their theoretical scheme would mean in practice to this one building—with quite devastating effect. The staff of my own school drew up a fifteen foolscap page memorandum of what the effect would be on their school, subject by subject, aspect by aspect, and a deputation of six senior men asked to be received by the sub-committee. They were, and in a series of meetings talked for a period of eight solid hours, expounding every section of this fearsome indictment. Full marks to the sub-committee for listening—this was consultation at its best. This and other meetings completely opened their eyes to what their scheme meant in terms of children, teachers, and schools. It was interesting to watch their assurance and determination fade away. By the time the Director produced his next Report in January 1966, his pet scheme was quite dead, and everyone knew it.

It was given a decent burial. There was a solemn rehearsal of how it would have operated in detail, if it had lived that long, with twelve pages of numerical analysis and statistical tables—all a shocking waste of somebody's valuable time. I imagine they had been prepared with loving care before the chopper fell, and it was felt they might as well see the light of day. But the fundamental disadvantages of this scheme—so cruelly exposed by the informed opposition of the united body of teachers—were now written into this document. Heresy had again become holy writ. A half-hearted attempt was made to consider two similar schemes, involving middle schools from 11+ to 13+, and from 10+ to 13+, but it was already known what the teachers would say about these if they were ever asked. 'A two-tier system with transfer at 13+', the document gloomily concluded, 'whether entry to the first tier be at 10 or 11 creates more problems without solving all the difficulties of a two-tier system with transfer at 14.' This was the end of the road.

But was it? There came a sudden flash of administrative brilliance, or desperation, or maybe by a process of elimination it was the only possibility left. We had talked about 10+, 11+, 13+, and 14+. There was only one figure that had been missed out. What, if anything, could be done with 12+? All the facts and figures and statistical tables had been worked out for these other schemes. It was suddenly noticed that if one rearranged them with 12+ as a starting-point, the simple arithmetic of it all clicked into place far better than it had ever done before. If one deferred the age of transfer from primary to secondary schools till 12 +, one could, in theory at least, organize secondary education throughout the city on the basis of five fully comprehensive schools taking pupils from 12 + to 18 +. This suggestion was hopefully attached to the Director's Report of January 1966 under the heading of 'A Further Alternative', and was worked out in considerable detail in a further Report entirely devoted to it in April of the same year. We were off on the merry-go-round of yet another scheme.

But this time there was a subtle difference.

If, in the light of this report and the representations that they have received from the teachers (says the concluding paragraph of the Director's January Report), the Sub-Committee are of the opinion that the scheme based on 12+ transfer merits serious follow up, I would suggest that such a scheme be referred to the teachers' associations for their observations and to the Department of Education and Science so that it can be considered by the Department at a semi-official level before an 'official' scheme is finally drawn up.

It may have been little more than a Freudian slip that the local teachers took precedence in his mind over the Department of Education and Science, but slips of this kind are most revealing. Real attention was now being paid to what we had to say. We had come a long way from the time when we were sitting disconsolately on the side-lines, feeling neglected and unimportant.

But first, let us get the Department of Education and Science out of the way. They were by this time under great pressure to alter their original ruling on the age of transfer, since many other areas had started pressing for the essential elbow-room that this gave. Circular 13/66 of May 1966 finally legalized ages of transfer other than 11 +, though official resistance had crumbled well before this time. But how many authorities had already got themselves so firmly committed to questionable two-tier schemes that it was now too late for them to take advantage of this elbow-room? It was the sturdy opposition of the teachers which alone had prevented our area being in this category, and for this if for nothing else their efforts had been worthwhile.

I will not trouble you with a detailed account of how we

considered from every angle the Director's new proposals, but gradually teacher opinion began to clarify, and after many hours of impassioned debate amongst the various associations, the Teachers' Panel was able to present another unanimous statement, speaking once again for all teachers. This was a much more meaty and detailed affair than anything we had so far produced, which was a clear sign that teachers, who formerly could only agree on broad general principles, were now in much closer agreement on the details of the implementation of any comprehensive scheme. The statement started by paying tribute to the careful consideration which had been given to what we had had to say about the previous two-tier scheme, and acknowledged that the present scheme was a genuine attempt to remove some of the principal difficulties we had pointed out. But it introduced fresh complications of its own.

For instance, we had no opposition at all in principle to changing the transfer age from primary to secondary schools from 11 to 12. Indeed, we strongly welcomed it in principle, since it now made necessary a close study of primary education in the city, which had so far tended to be ignored whilst all eyes were on the secondary schools. We also saw the powerful argument of administrative expediency behind this change. The numbers of children did fit better into the existing schools, and when it came to providing extra places it was markedly cheaper to provide extra places in primary schools rather than in secondary schools. But as teachers we felt that administrative expediency must also be supported by direct and demonstrable educational advantages to the children before we could be fully happy about the proposed change. How would it all work in practice? It was not good enough just to stick an extra year on to the primary stage, and allow the children to mark time. The entire pattern of the infant and junior schools must be recast so that this year became an integral part of a continuous process, at the end of which boys and girls of all ranges of ability had not only reached the standard they would have attained at the end of their first year in the secondary school had they transferred at 11+, but in certain important respects had markedly improved on this standard. Anything less than this would savour of change for change's sake rather than real progress. We then pointed out that all this meant that primary schools would in future have to have access for their older pupils to junior laboratories, gymnasia, games-fields etc., which they now got when they entered secondary schools at 11; and this led to a detailed attack on the official accommodation schedules and 'pricing' of this part of the scheme.

Now if a good deal more money was to be spent on primary schools—as we submitted it must be—there would be even less available for secondary reorganization, and this meant that the proper utilization of the existing buildings was even more important than in previous schemes. We were, it seems, to have five comprehensive secondary schools catering for all pupils from 12 + to 18 +, but what did it mean in practice? One of these new schools was to be formed by amalgamating three separate and well-appointed schools on the same campus, and this we conceded would make a viable comprehensive community— though there were difficulties even here, which we enumerated. As to the other four suggested schools, they were quite unacceptable. In two cases they would be too small to be viable. The other two were to be made up to very large establishments by spatchcocking together in one case three, and in the other case four, separate schools, which were quite distant from each other. These two complexes, we felt, could never be knit together to form proper comprehensive communities. We tried to visualize some of the problems of time-tabling and organization with which the heads of these complexes would be faced, noting in passing that one of them would be faced with the strange anomaly of single sex education in a co-educational school. Moreover, we pointed out that the present scheme called for all secondary schools to be co-educational, which again limited parental choice. By nominating which primary schools would feed to which comprehensive the scheme would create area schools with rigidly defined catchment areas, and again would do away with the parent's right to send his child to a school in some other part of the city. We bitterly attacked the Appendix to the Director's Report in which he set out the phased introduction of this scheme; this was clearly an arithmetical administrative exercise paying no regard to the interests of the children concerned. For instance, G.C.E. and C.S.E. pupils would have been whipped away to strange schools less than nine months before they took their examinations; and year groups would have been arbitrarily split up between different schools; in the case of one school it would have to split up one age group of its pupils and dispatch one section to a boys' school, one to a girls' school, and a third to a co-educational school. For good measure, we added a statistical appendix of our own in which we analysed in detail the expected size of the sixth forms in these five comprehensive schools. We were able to brush aside what the planners claimed to see in their crystal ball, and show without fear of contradiction the disastrous effect that splitting up the academic sixth forms between these five comprehensive schools was going to have. It would lead to such small numbers in every case but one that it would be quite impossible to retain the present alternative courses available, let alone add to them, and would have set back sixth form development in the city to where it had been more than a generation ago. This, we felt, could hardly be intended.

We ended by regretting that so much that we had to say sounded destructive, when in fact we wanted to be constructive. This we blamed on the system.

The present pattern of negotiations under which a scheme is put up in a fair amount of detail without any teacher participation in the early stages of its formulation is not the happiest of arrangements. Teacher organizations then find themselves in the position of having to 'knock it down' to secure acceptance of fundamental educational principles which should have been given greater emphasis at an earlier stage. It would not be easy to devise machinery for this, but if it did prove possible it would be a great step forward. The crux of the problem as we see it is that no scheme for the future, however good, should be introduced in such a way that it jeopardizes the education of the children at present passing through the schools; and equally that no scheme for the future should be accepted merely because it seems administratively possible to introduce it quickly and cheaply, so that it can be said that 'action has been taken', but it must be a scheme which clearly and demonstrably constitutes a marked educational and social improvement for all the children in our schools, and gives our teachers the conditions in which they can do a first rate professional job, equal to that done anywhere else in the country. Responsible administrators, such as we believe the Education Committee to be, are clearly aware that if you will the end you must also will the means, and that the state of the national economy is so markedly limiting the means that it must also powerfully influence the rate at which real progress can be made towards these ends. A genuine 'Fabian approach' to their problems would seem to be indicated.

This was all so obviously sensible that they took our advice. A meeting of the full Joint Advisory Council was called to consider our observations, but in completely different circumstances to the last one. For one thing, it was not preceded by stormy scenes in public as the last one had been. Nor was it necessary to use this meeting to drive unacceptable thoughts into deaf ears, as on the previous occasion. The advance copies of our statement, which out of courtesy we had provided, had already done our work for us, and in a matter of days a revised scheme emerged which was intended to take care of our principal criticisms.

12 + as the age of transfer was to stand, but every effort was to be made to improve the facilities in the primary schools on the lines which we had indicated. The final scheme still envisaged five fully comprehensive schools accommodating all children from 12+ to 18+, but it was accepted that it might be a good many years before this came about. In the meantime an interim scheme would operate, which would avoid setting up the unwieldy complexes of which we had complained, and would also avoid the division of sixth formers into absurdly small groups. The three schools on the one campus—which we had conceded could make one all-through comprehensive school—would be amalgamated to form such a school. The girls' grammar school and the boys' grammar school, after the essential rebuilding, would become fairly small comprehensive and co-educational schools, with fairly large sixth form accommodation. There were to be four other comprehensive schools retaining their pupils from 12 to 16, but sending their prospective sixth formers along to the schools with existing sixth forms. Over the years, as sixth form numbers increased and rebuilding allowed, these four schools would unite as two schools retaining their pupils till 18+, and having their own sixth forms. Elaborate steps were to be taken to see that none of these schools developed as an area school, but rather served the city as a whole. Care was to be taken to see that each school had a full spread of ability roughly in accordance with the distribution of ability throughout the

population, and so far as possible parents were to be allowed to choose the school to which they wished to send their child. A computer would be sworn in to help make this delicate balance between 'Parents' wishes' on the one hand, and a 'full spread of ability' on the other. How well, or badly, this will operate is a matter of opinion, as indeed is so much else about this new scheme. So a working party of teachers was to be convened to go into the detailed planning of the scheme, and advise the committee as to its viability as the details emerge. This 'Revised Version' was adopted by the sub-committee on July 22nd 1966, and by the City Council at its October meeting in the same year. It was exactly two years and four months since the Director had presented his first Report on this subject—hard slogging months and years, when tragedy jostled with triumph, and laughter was mixed with tears—but at long last the City had its Plan.

INTERNAL REORGANIZATION

In the previous chapter, I have concentrated on giving a detailed account of the machinery of consultation which had first of all to be created and then used before the simple statement that the City was to 'Go Comprehensive' could be defined and clarified into a practical policy. I have said little of the genuine emotions, prejudices, and ideals which were involved at every stage, because these tend to take the limelight at the time, and divert attention from the more humdrum work which has to take place. I would not suggest that the way we tackled it was perfect, or that the resultant compromise was fully satisfactory to anybody concerned; least of all would I claim that the pattern we worked out tells you how other authorities approached their similar problems. But I am certain that some such humdrum stage can only be missed out at great peril to the eventual success of any scheme proposed, and that authorities who took short-cuts and completely ignored views divergent to their own will live to regret it. We at least had all done our best to turn a slogan into a practical course of action. We had a plan.

But before that plan can start to become a reality, it will be necessary to alter the internal arrangements of every secondary school. Again, I would like to leave aside for the moment the genuine emotions, prejudices, and ideals, which tend to get all the attention, and concentrate on the basic machinery which it will be necessary to create inside the schools to turn them into comprehensive establishments.

They will be large—possibly not such mammoths as was once thought essential—but still much larger in sheer numbers of pupils than the normal grammar or secondary modern school to which we have become accustomed. Moreover, they will be larger than the numbers alone would seem to indicate for two reasons. Firstly, there will be a much wider spread of ability than we have been used to—stretching from the very bright child to the practically illiterate—and special arrangements will have to be made to provide the appropriate treatment for these, and all intermediate grades of ability, within the same school. Seconbly, their middle school will be swollen by many children who would not be in school at all if it were not for the raising of the school leaving age—and arrangements for these (often unwilling) pupils will add to the load. So as well as being large they will be complex, not to say confusing, places for the boy or girl entering them for the first time. The great curse of sheer size and complexity is that it is more difficult for the individual to know and be known, and this seems quite contrary to the comprehensive idea as I understand it—that the individual shall get greater attention and consideration, not less. How can this very real danger be avoided? Partly, I think, by giving careful thought to the basic administrative organization of the school.

On his first day in the overpoweringly large school, the child will find himself in a Form Unit of about thirty other children. Possibly a staggered start on the first day will help him get over his strangeness. It seems to be generally accepted that each of these groups will have been carefully selected beforehand to make sure that they are a social cross-section of the community, and that the group contains boys of the full range of ability. It is regarded as vital by many schools that this important mixture of both ability and social origin should not be left to chance, but others are not so sure that a more random way of forming the Form Unit isn't better after all. In any case, the child finds himself on his first day in a 'family group', and remains in the same group as he progresses through the school. In theory, the class teacher remains with the same Form Unit throughout its existence—though in practice this may very rarely be possible.

It is important, however, that the class teacher should maintain close contact with his group for as many years as possible, so that from close contact with it over a period of time he can build up an intimate knowledge of each individual child. The class teacher has certain obvious administrative duties. He marks the attendance register, maintains the pupil record cards, checks the homework diary, and so on. But he has more important functions than this. It is hoped that he will win the confidence of his group, and make sure that it lives in peace and harmony within itself and within the larger community. He is, in fact, a father figure, who restrains or encourages the members of his group, and does his best to ensure that each one develops as his potential allows.

The class teacher, of course, is founded on the traditional form master of a grammar school, and the connection is closer that many people will admit. Few grammar-school forms in my experience are as homogeneous as their critics or their friends would like to think. That is to say there is quite a marked range of ability between the top and bottom boy, and they are also a reasonable social cross-section. A good form master goes to endless trouble to get to know his boys, both inside the school and out, and the influence of good, conscientious form masters is the most powerful single influence for good in the traditional grammar schools. The same will be true of the new comprehensive schools. They will stand or fall on the calibre of the teachers who are put in charge of Form Units. They are the yeast who must leaven the lump. Their task will be even more difficult than that of the traditional form master. The form unit will not be a unit based on grades of intelligence or set programmes of lessons; it will be almost entirely a social unit, with all the ingredients of social disintegration built into it, and liable to fly apart if it is not carefully watched and tended. As it gets further up the school there will be less and less educational contact between its members in lesson times, and unless time is set apart for special group activities, it may become more and more unreal. If it loses its influence and power at the very time it is most needed it would tragically weaken the impact of the school on its pupils.

We have so far broken down the total intake of the school into form units of thirty pupils; we are now faced with fitting these groups of children into the group of buildings that is going to constitute the school. There are two main ways in which this can be done; usually, the buildings dictate which way can be chosen; and usually the solution chosen will be a mixture of certain interchangeable aspects of both ways.

The first depends on a mainly horizontal division of the school. One section of the building is set apart as the Junior School, another as the Middle School, and a third as the Senior School, which may or may not include the Sixth Form. Each section contains all the children in the form units of the appropriate years, and each section has its own sectional Head and Deputy Head. The Head of the Junior School, for instance, is responsible for the progress and well-being of all the junior members of the school, and under the general guidance of the Headmaster of the school, carries out many of the functions of an independent headmaster. He would correspond with parents and arrange interviews with them. He would take the Morning Assembly of the Junior School, and settle all the routine matters affecting the junior children without having to refer them to the overall Headmaster. If he is to do all this, he must be relieved from a good part of his teaching duties, and be provided with his own room and clerical assistance. A good deal is known about this fairly traditional sub-division of a large school, so there is no new principle involved. In practice, the Heads of the three sections can exert an enormous influence on the smooth running of their own section in particular, and of the whole school in general.

The second depends on a mainly vertical division of the school. The pupils are arranged in Houses, each House containing 200 or so children, drawn from all age groups and all ability levels throughout the school. When he enters the school, instead of becoming a member of a 'horizontal' form unit, the child may well be placed in a 'vertical' Tutor Group, each Tutor Group containing a proportion of children of all ages from the youngest to the oldest. The House is then composed of a certain number of these Tutor Groups, a child remaining in the same Tutor Group and the same House throughout his school career. Each House is put in the charge of a Head of House and his Deputy, the Head of House in this case being equivalent to the Junior, Middle, or Senior School Head under the previous scheme.

Ideally, he needs his own room and clerical assistance, and a reduced teaching programme to enable him to operate his House efficiently. There should be some building which clearly belongs to the House, containing an assembly hall sufficient to accommodate all members of the House, a dining-room and kitchens so that the House can eat as a unit, and a staff-room for the members of staff who are closely connected with this particular House. Certainly, if the buildings are such that a House has not got its own geographical location and physical existence, and the children cannot in some measure feel that they 'live' there, it will remain an artificial concept, and it will be difficult to get them to take House loyalties seriously. The House idea once again is a traditional idea, borrowed with certain important variants from the traditional Public School. The most important variant is, of course, that pupils in a Public School are actually resident in their House, whereas in a day school they are not. Provided this difficulty can be overcome in such a way that the child feels that the membership of a House is natural and sensible, there is no doubt that a house-master can be a far more powerful and influential person than he has usually been in the past in day schools in this country. Exactly how he will function will vary from school to school. In some schools, the junior children will go into special lower school houses for the first year or two, before transferring to the House itself. In other schools the Sixth Form will be organized separately, so that the Fifth Formers would be the senior members of the Houses, and would have a chance of assuming responsibility. As always, the human factor is important, and the House will be as good as the house-master's personality and initiative allow it to be. If he is very good, then he will build up powerful House loyalties, and his work will have been success-ful—but with one proviso. If the children dine and live as a unit, if the staff in the House have their own separate staff-room, a dangerous tendency may develop for the House to become everything and the School nothing. There is a certain danger that you can be too successful in splitting up the school into Houses, and some horizontal organization is essential right across the Houses to make sure that the vertical splits do not become too complete and permanent; more regular Morning Assemblies for the whole school might help, for instance.

But whether your principal administrative division is vertical, horizontal, or a mixture of the two, it is clear that the problem of communications in a large school of this kind is going to be greater than in the past. Instead of one Morning Assembly at the end of which notices can be given out to the entire school, there will be several assemblies, and the same notice repeated with different inflexions in different places to different groups tends inexorably to turn into several different notices. Because of the larger and more scattered buildings, and the essential internal divisions I have just mentioned, it will be physically more difficult for master to contact master, or to winkle out a particular pupil for some special activity. If, for instance, you are arranging a cricket practice at fairly short notice, and need to get a message to several reserves, the sheer size of the school and the complications of its time-table can turn a simple task into a very laborious process. This sort of problem exists in all schools, but it will be multiplied many times in these larger schools, most of which will not have been designed to make this easy. It will be up to the Headmaster to see that an efficient machine of communications, operating down from the Headmaster to the school, and back up from the school to the Headmaster, is established; and the great danger is, of course, that well-oiled machines tend to act in a machine-like way. A great deal will depend on the personality and wisdom of the Headmaster, who must see to it that humanity and flexibility are retained in what by its very nature must tend to become a dehumanized, committee-run establishment. He must delegate his responsibilities in a way he has seldom done in the past, and may run some danger of turning into a rather grey, remote, administrative figure. But great headmasters of large schools have the knack of still being able to impress their personality on everyone committed to their charge, and it is their beneficent influence which permeates the entire school. Clearly the wholesale introduction of large comprehensive schools will call for an inexhaustible supply of 'great' headmasters, and these are in notoriously short supply.

Apart from the changes in administrative organization which we have been considering, the pattern of teaching will also have to be changed, and this is probably even more important as far as the impact on pupils is concerned. There seem to be five clearly defined phases through which the pupils of all schools will pass. As they enter the school there will be a 'foundation period', possibly lasting for a year. During this time the object will be to enable the pupils to settle down and become acclimatized to the school, and to enable the school to get to know their new pupils and their potentialities. The 'foundation period' will merge into the next phase, when in theory all children will follow a common course, since one of the basic ideas of a comprehensive school is that it should postpone 'selection' as long as possible, and keep all options open for all children. For precisely how long this can be done, or should be done, is a matter of opinion; but however firmly the school sets its face against premature selection the process will be inexorably going on. By this I mean that there will be a process of continuous selection or self-differentiation going on, as one child separates himself from another by his differing speed, competence, and interests. The school cannot afford to ignore this natural process—indeed, it would be a very bad school if it even tried to do so. In the middle school phase, therefore, important differences will arise in the curriculum of children. All abilities may continue to be taught together for some things, but different subjects or different integrated courses will be available for different children, and these subjects or courses will be taught at different levels according to the requirements of the pupils. For instance, all children will be taught science during the middle school phase, but this will mean vastly different things according to the group in which the child is being taught. The middle school phase will merge into the period when the first external examinations (the 'O' Level G.C.E. and the C.S.E.) become important. A most complex time-table will have emerged by this time. Some pupils will be offering a wide selection of 'O' Level subjects—but the combination of these subjects will be different in individual cases. Some pupils will be offering a mixture of G.C.E. and C.S.E. subjects—and again there will be marked variation in the actual subjects. Some pupils will be offering only C.S.E. subjects, and some will not be taking part in any external examination at all. Now whatever you may think of external examinations, there is little point in entering candidates unless they have been properly prepared, and in many subjects it is essential that they should have been working on the appropriate syllabus for a period of at least two years before they take the examination, and in some cases for longer than this. The temptation then is to guide pupils towards the appropriate syllabus, and subject, and course, as early as possible; which is in direct contradiction to the doctrinal theory that all options must be kept open for all children as long as possible. How long is 'possible'? This is the conundrum facing each headmaster, and it is a question which might well have baffled Solomon. The final phase—and it is hoped that there will be a great increase of boys and girls from 16 to 18 years of age who will stay at school for it—is what is now called the Sixth Form. It is clear that there will be changes in what is meant by this term, and it may even be more honest to stop using this phrase altogether, except as meaning that a pupil is in the sixth year of his secondary course. Many pupils, in some cases the majority of pupils, in the first year of a comprehensive sixth form will be pupils who are in fact simply spending a sixth year in the school, possibly to take some 'O' Level G.C.E. subjects, or some C.S.E. subjects for which they were not ready the previous year; or they may be pupils who have never considered taking any external examination at all, and simply wish to continue with elementary instruction until they are mature enough to go out into the world. There is much to be said for encouraging children such as this who have developed more slowly to stay at school for a further period, though what they do in this time will bear little resemblance to traditional sixth form studies. There will, of course, be a nucleus of traditional academic sixth formers, with their eyes set on the 'A' Level of the G.C.E., followed by entrance to universities or the professions. The size of this group is crucial since it has an important bearing on the variety of academic courses which can be economically provided within the school. A smaller academic sixth must necessarily mean either a restriction on the subjects available—or an uneconomic use of scarce teachers—or possibly both together. It will, of course, be necessary to integrate in some way these academic sixth formers with the larger numbers (possibly the majority) of pupils who have stayed at school for a sixth or seventh year with vastly different objectives; and here experience in the earlier years in the school, and attitudes built up in Form Units and Tutor Groups will be invaluable. But it is still a large problem. The grammar-school sixth form has been one of the glorious successes of English education; it would be foolish to expect that you can radically alter its intake and broaden its objectives without turning it into a very different thing. However, the grammar-school sixth form is not a static affair, and in the natural course of events is altering all the time. Indeed, its strongest advocates would, in the same breath, give you a list of the changes they would like to see in it. But the rapid, drastic, and sudden change which the comprehensive reorganization of all secondary schools will bring about is of a totally different order, and will need to be carefully watched if the traditional virtues of what we now understand as sixth-form education are not to be lost. The danger is that in trying to make these virtues available to all one will only succeed in getting rid of them altogether.

During these five phases of school life, the actual teaching groups themselves will be determined, in theory, on one or other of two mutually exclusive principles, though in practice, whatever may be said officially, it is very unlikely that any school will rely on one of these principles to the complete exclusion of the other. We are much more likely to find a 'mixed economy', a compromise between the two extremes. But in theory at least, there will be a direct choice between the streamed school, and the unstreamed school.

There is no doubt that the streamed school will lead to a smoother and quieter transition from secondary schools as we know them today—and with so much upheaval going on there is much to be said, particularly from the point of view of the children in the schools at present, for sparing them from any unnecessary change. The idea of streaming—that is to say arranging for all children in a class to be of roughly comparable ability—is said to spring from the psychological theories current at the time of the Hadow and Spens Reports. These theories said that children were born with a fixed, and measurable, amount of intelligence, and since this was largely unchangeable, it should in theory be possible to put children in their appropriate schools and streams on the basis of an incontrovertible and unalterable Intelligence Quotient. More recent psychologists have shown that their predecessors were talking nonsense— casting doubt on whether it is possible to isolate any one thing

95

which can be called 'intelligence', and proving that if one can do this it certainly is not a constant factor. Therefore, they argue, streaming is both impossible and immoral.

Now I know few practical teachers who swallowed hook, line, and sinker, the psychological theories popular at the time of the Hadow and Spens Reports, and anyone working in schools had spotted the element of nonsense in them long before the next wave of psychologists came along to disprove them. A school is grateful for such help as can be provided from such expert sources, but cannot abdicate its responsibilities in their favour, particularly its fundamental duty of studying and understanding its pupils. Contact with them in the class-room underlines how useless the concept of an abstract quality called intelligence is, since we are constantly meeting children who show aptitude and interest in one subject, and have difficulty with another. Again, it would be a policy of despair to accept for one moment that a child's abilities are incapable of being improved within certain limits, since the whole art of class-room teaching is to help children to do better than either they or anybody else expected them to do.

Streaming, in fact, was known in schools long before the psychological advisers to Hadow and Spens arrived to elevate it to a theory. It was a practical teaching device to get out of a particular set of difficulties. When there were large numbers of children and a shortage of teachers, it was easier to handle the over-large classes which resulted if it could be arranged that the class was reasonably homogeneous; and it was physically impossible for the teacher to give anything like the necessary individual or group attention to the same over-size class if it contained too wide a spread of ability. Streaming has many disadvantages—and when too rigidly operated these can do great harm—but for many years to come it is a device which to a greater or a lesser extent will find a place in many of our secondary schools.

It seems likely that schools retaining streaming will collate all the information available to them from the primary schools, together with their own findings about the children's abilities and aptitudes during the 'foundation period', and arrange the children in three broad bands of ability. The first ability band will contain all the children likely at some future date to be concerned with external examinations, either G.C.E. or C.S.E. It is important that in the early years this ability band should be as all inclusive as is realistically possible. The second ability band will contain the children unlikely to be concerned with external examinations in the future, for whom a completely 'school based' syllabus freed from the restrictive pressures of external examining bodies is most suitable. The third ability band would, we hope, be a small one, containing those children whose progress so far has been so poor that they need special remedial treatment.

Now the way in which the school treats this third ability band would seem to me to be the acid test of whether or not it is achieving comprehensive education. If it does a first class job with these children it will almost certainly have got its social and educational priorities right throughout the rest of the school. Some of them will be of such limited intelligence that any progress they ever make will be minimal; but the majority of them will have a higher potential than they have ever so far been able to show, and will have been held back by grave handicaps—shocking home conditions, physical or temperamental peculiarities, long illnesses, psychological blockages, etc. —which more fortunate children have escaped. They are markedly insecure in, and suspicious of, what they have so far found to be a hostile world. They have so far failed, and have no in-built urge to try again. To pretend this problem does not exist, and to expect them to hold their own in a mixed ability group in a strange large school, on the theoretical grounds that segregation of any kind must not be allowed to exist, seems to me quite wrong. They must have a room, or rooms, of their own, in which most, though not all, of their instruction will take place— because of the simple practical point that such children find moving around from place to place in large crowded buildings both confusing and distracting. Most of their work must be done under the guidance of one person, specially trained to ensure that some success, however small, results from their efforts, since it is only on the basis of small successes that a start can be made to build up confidence and a feeling that it is worth making further efforts. I say it is important that they should work under the guidance of one person because, again, such children find difficulty in making contact with adults, and a variety of teachers during the week can be confusing to them. But this does not mean that this one person should be the only person in the school showing an interest in them. For instance, there seems to me to be a golden opportunity for sympathetic and interested sixth formers to spend a short time each week working with the remedial group as a form of social service. It would have the practical advantage of providing, under the guidance of the specialist teacher, for individual attention for these children, in a way which even a generous staffing ratio would not make possible. It would have a marked therapeutic effect on the remedial children in proving to them that other children cared about them—since the normal lot of the backward child so often follows the pattern of partial rejection by its parents, more complete rejection by society, and total and cruel rejection by its more normal contemporaries. It would clearly establish the philosophy of the school—that to those whose need is greatest, the most attention must be given—and from those whose ability is greatest, society expects the largest contribution. In separating these remedial children from the main-stream of school life, it is important at all times to remember why this is being done. The sole object should be to overcome the special difficulties of these children, so that as soon as possible they can return to the main-stream with sufficient confidence and competence to survive in it; and a really successful remedial class is one whose last pupil has just left it for the main school.

Similarly, for the second ability band, those children unlikely to be concerned with external examinations, there is everything to be said for making it plain from the very start that their position in this group does not divide them either finally or completely, from the children in the first ability band. Not completely, since from the word go, the good school will see that wherever and whenever possible, in social and sporting activity, in House co-operation and competition, these two ability bands are closely integrated. Not finally, since the opportunity must always exist for a pupil who progresses better than expected to be moved on to a C.S.E. course in the appropriate subject or subjects. But when this has been allowed for, there is a great deal to be said for treating them as a coherent group, working on flexible elementary courses, designed to allow them to succeed in attaining modest targets, rather than condemning them to more ambitious objectives in which they are certain to fail. Or rather, we should substitute appropriate ambitions for the inappropriate pursuit of external examination certificates. It is important that all children should be helped in school to develop certain skills of communication in speech and writing, in reading with understanding and discrimination, and in calculations involving numbers and measurement, since these are basic skills, and without them they will be cut off from much human thought and experience. But some children learn these skills slowly and with difficulty, and the danger is that they will spend their whole time at school in mechanically trying to improve these skills, and never have an opportunity to use them. They may be kept busy, but never have their minds and imaginations fully extended. Since they do not acquire factual knowledge easily, and tend to forget it quickly, there is a dangerous tendency to over-simplify and limit the subject-matter, so that the range of information and ideas to which they are introduced can be seriously inadequate. The effect of this is that they are educationally undernourished, and it is hardly surprising that boredom and lack of effort follow. Is it possible to work out for pupils of only moderate skills a syllabus with the sort of content which will exercise their minds and emotions and feed their imaginations? Most certainly. The Newsom Report, for instance, concentrates on showing how this can be done:

In short, we are saying that whatever lessons appear on the time-table, it is essential that the pupils be helped and stimulated by them to enlarge their understanding and practise their skills; that some direct experience, which can mean, for example, listening to a broadcast or watching a film, as well as actively doing or making things, will often provide the most effective starting point for discussion; and that from this they can advance to some critical evaluation, perhaps a search for further knowledge, and to making some written record, where this is appropriate, of what they have been doing. All of this bears a good deal of resemblance, we are aware, to the experience of learning offered in a lively junior school. The main difference at this secondary stage will be that there will be a need to deal with more mature interests and more subtle judgments, and to make more explicit the connections between what is done in one subject and another.

The object of separating these children into a 'second ability band' is to make it easier to concentrate attention on their very real needs; to see that more demands are made on them in both the nature and in the amount of work required, not less; to stimulate intellectual and imaginative effort, and to extend the pupils' range of ideas in order to bring about a fuller and more lasting literacy; and to ensure that basic skills in reading, writing and calculation should be used and strengthened through every medium in the curriculum.

The first ability band, containing all those likely to be concerned with external examinations, will in a large school contain children of a wide spread of ability, ranging from the bright G.C.E. candidates to the quite doubtful C.S.E. possibles, and this of itself will ensure that the teaching groups in this band in the early years will be groups of quite mixed ability. There will, however, be an in-built guarantee that the abilities at the top and bottom of the teaching group are not so grotesquely wide apart that communication between them is so difficult as to be almost impossible. As the children reach the middle school, their differing rate of progress and varying interests in subjects will call for ability setting, and a more definite division into those children preparing for 'O' Level only, those preparing for a mixture of 'O' Level and C.S.E., and those concentrating on C.S.E. only. This may seem an awkward and unnecessary division, particularly as it will have to be superimposed on another more basic division of the subjects a child is presenting for examination purposes, which will vary from child to child. Clearly, it is awkward and unnecessary, and it cannot be long before some merger takes place between 'O' Level G.C.E. and the C.S.E., so that schools may retain more flexibility at this stage. Possibly, too, the insistence on the overall importance of success in external examinations at this stage of a reasonably bright pupil's life will be reduced, and greater emphasis given to the school's duty to provide a general, all-round education at this stage, which will stimulate, extend, and encourage bright children to more specialized and intensive study at a later stage.

But all this, say the advocates of the unstreamed school, is merely evading the issue. Your streamed comprehensive school, they say, is simply the old tripartite system, thinly disguised by substituting one headmaster for three, and one school building for several separate schools—but still the old system. They call for a much more radical approach, basing themselves on the encouraging experience of many forward-looking junior schools. Separate primary schools had come into existence as a result of the Hadow Report (1931), and this Report had given a clear lead on the desirability of streaming in these schools:

The break at 11 has rendered possible a more thorough classification of children. It is important that this opportunity should be turned to fullest account. One great advantage of the self-contained primary school is that the teachers have special opportunities for making a suitable classification of the children according to their natural gifts and abilities. . . . In general, we agree with our psychological witnesses in thinking that in very large primary schools there might, wherever possible, be a 'triple track' system of organization, viz.: a series of 'A' classes for the bright children, and a series of smaller 'C' classes or groups to include retarded children, both series being parallel to the ordinary series of 'B' classes or groups for the average children.

But in the early 1950s this practice began to be criticized, on the grounds that it tended to exaggerate the original differences rather than to reduce them, and that children in 'B' and 'C' streams put up the kind of indifferent performances which seemed to be expected from such forms. It seemed far better to arrange the children in classes of mixed ability which would avoid this, provided one got away from the idea of the class being the only, or even the major, teaching unit. Much more emphasis could then be given to individual work or group activity, and one might then achieve the exciting paradox of a constant, united effort by children of widely varying ability, one helping the other, and also the freedom for individual children to progress at the rate best fitted to their individual abilities. Experiments in junior schools have shown that there is a great deal to be said for this approach, and it is increasingly used in primary schools these days. Why should it be supposed that it completely loses its value at 11 + or 12 + when a child moves on to a secondary school? Isn't it time that secondary schools broke with the traditional arrangements of the grammar and public schools, and paid attention to what the Newsom Report called 'the experience of learning in a lively junior school'?

Let us begin then, with unstreamed, mixed ability groups as the basic teaching unit in our comprehensive school. It may be that later in the school one has to start setting pupils for certain subjects which they are offering for external examinations, and 'ability grouping', or 'setting', or 'streaming', call it what you will, may slip in by the back-door; but as far as possible, as a matter of policy, one endeavours to see that children continue to be taught in mixed ability groups. This will lead to greater unity within the school—since one has got rid of the tripartite division of ability bands. It will still be necessary, of course, to solve the basic problem of an unstreamed class, whether it is in a primary or a secondary school. It is merely a negative move to lump children of all abilities in one class, if one cannot take positive steps to see that it leads to a situation where individual learning is encouraged. As the Plowden Report says of Junior Schools, though it is largely applicable to the early years of Secondary Schools:

If class teaching plays a large part, the abler children will be held back and the slower will lose heart. Clear-cut streaming within a class can be more damaging to children than streaming within a school. There must be groups, of course, based sometimes on interest and sometimes on achievement, but they should change in accordance with the children's needs. One difficulty in the unstreamed class will certainly be to provide for the very able and for the slower learners. The slower children can gain from the enthusiasm and interests of the able children but only if the teacher sees that the slow children are absorbed into the class community and into small groups, and given praise, attention and instruction enough to encourage them to fresh effort. For the able children much more can be done by making accessible, in the class-room and the school as a whole, a liberal range of books and other equipment, though they ought sometimes to be fired and challenged by working with like-minded children from another class. Checks will be needed that children are working to their capacity. Careful individual records are essential. Schemes for the whole school will need to be in every class-room and classes, as well as individuals, ought to have records which show, for example, the literature that has been read to them and the interests which have provided a point of departure for the class as a whole or for substantial groups within it.

Clearly the handling of these mixed ability groups in senior schools will call for unusually adaptable and resourceful teachers, and the work will be tremendously tiring. Conventional class-rooms will be quite inadequate to cope with the requirements of such work, and school architecture will have to become equally elastic and accommodating. It may well be that the inadequacies of any one room, and any one teacher, will lead to the introduction of 'team teaching' in a suite of rooms to provide the greater flexibility required. Will the general all-round attainment suffer by abolishing streaming from secondary schools? It does not appear to have done in junior schools which have successfully experimented with this approach—though less is heard from junior schools whose experiments have been less successful. But how far can experience in junior schools be strictly relevant to the problems of secondary schools, where the natural keenness and will to please of the the pre-adolescent has been replaced by the shy, awkward reluctance of the adolescent? How much of the shy awkward reluctance would disappear in an unstreamed comprehensive school, whose basic philosophy genuinely was based on co-operation rather than competition? Would it, as the cynics maintain, still be very much the mixture as before— the keen still keen, the lazy still lazy?

Now the surprising thing, the alarming thing, is that there has been insufficient research to give definite answers to these and other questions asked in this chapter, and such experience as there has been is inconclusive and at times contradictory. Yet we are pressing ahead with the internal reorganization of our secondary schools at a merry rate, and if some of the solutions are right, some will certainly be wrong. In a scientific age, it seems a remarkably hit-and-miss and unscientific means of proceeding. Properly evaluated pilot schemes might have been distinctly useful, so that so much was not left to chance, or to individual intuition. Certainly, as one who has to thread his way through the complicated maze of possibilities and alternatives I have just been outlining, I would have welcomed more authoritative guidance. It is easy to state what we are aiming at:

A school is not merely a teaching shop, it must transmit values and attitudes. It is a community in which children learn to live first and foremost as children and not as future adults. In family life children learn to live with people of all ages. The school sets out deliberately to devise the right environment for children, to allow them to be themselves and to develop in the way and at the pace appropriate to them. It tries to equalize opportunities and to compensate for handicaps. It lays special stress on individual discovery, on first hand experience and on opportunities for creative work. It insists that knowledge does not fall into neatly separate compartments and that work and play are not opposite but complementary. A child brought up in such an atmosphere at all stages of his education has some hope of becoming a balanced and mature adult and of being able to live in, to contribute to, and to look critically at the society of which he forms a part.

That is Plowden talking about primary schools, but it puts in a nutshell what all good secondary schools—grammar, technical, and modern—have been striving to be since the 1944 Act; and indicates what all comprehensive secondary schools must achieve for themselves in the future. But precisely how? The argument continues!

4

The Expectations

THE CLASSLESS SOCIETY

I have spent a good deal of time in the last chapter trying to
indicate some of the possible ways in which the group of
buildings and of children which an authority designates as a
comprehensive school will have to be organized; and this internal organization is vital if the school is to be 'not merely a
teaching shop' but a comprehensive 'community'. Shall it be
arranged in year groups or houses—horizontally or vertically—
shall it be streamed or unstreamed—and how does one cater
for the individual and at the same time maintain the unity of
the group, bring on the laggards without holding back the
bright? You may have found all this a little confusing, and
wonder why I have been so vague and non-committal. It is
because, as I said at the end of the last chapter, the argument
continues. So much of it is still a matter of opinion and personal
prejudice, since detailed research on the most satisfactory way
to arrange the internal organization of a comprehensive school
has just not been done. Indeed, it would be fair to say that it
has only just started.

Why then the rush? Why can't we wait for the fundamental
research to present us with a blue-print for the ideal organization of an ideal school of an ideal size offering the right opportunities for every child, and then get our authorities to build
and staff the appropriate schools? In its extreme form, this
question is tantamount to saying, 'Stop the world, I want to get
off', and is quite absurd. But there is an element of truth in it,
and there is no doubt that it would have been safer and saner

to plan and phase the whole operation from the beginning so that firmly based and thoroughly tested educational theory could go hand in hand with the increased provision of manpower and buildings, and thus ensure that comprehensive reorganization was a reality, rather than, as in many cases, a hollow sham. It will be a bitter disappointment to many parents, and many teachers, to find that for an indefinite time after 'vesting day' the great transformation has not done much more than alter the name at the door of the school. This will not be through lack of goodwill and effort on anybody's part, but is inherent in the harsh realities of the situation.

But the rush—the pressure for change—is social and political —and is impatient and intolerant of the economic and educational difficulties which stand between it and the ends it hopes to achieve. I do not, myself, see that there is anything wrong in the properly constituted democratic bodies deciding in broad general terms what the ends are which they expect the state schools to achieve—indeed, they would be neglecting their duty if they did not. But, apart from insisting that they must will the means as well as willing the ends, it would also be helpful if the ends themselves were expressed more clearly, logically, and unequivocally, than has so far been done. As far as I can see, however, there are three matters about which the people of this country (of all political parties and of none) are concerned, and they hope that comprehensive schools will provide a better answer to these than the existing tripartite system has done. First, there is an uncomfortable feeling abroad that there is much wasted talent amongst our children, pools of ability so far untapped, which must be quickly utilized for the economic health and well-being of our country in an increasingly technological civilization. Secondly, there is a strong egalitarian feeling, which is becoming more and more widespread, which feels that it is immoral to be satisfied with any system of schools which does not guarantee equality of opportunity to all children. Thirdly, there are social reformers in our midst who are dissatisfied with our class-ridden society, and wish to use the state schools as a battering-ram to break down these outmoded distinctions, and introduce a new classless society. We must examine these three points in some detail, to see what is meant by them, and whether it is going to be possible to deal with them more satisfactorily by the new system of schools than by the old.

Before we can discuss the relationship between schools and class, however, there are one or two obvious points that should be made clear. I say 'obvious', but it is quite remarkable how often the polemicists can manage to disregard them. They manage, for instance, to give the impression that our present schools are class-conscious institutions which are largely responsible for maintaining, and in fact did a great deal to create, the class divisions in society, and if they were destroyed (particularly the grammar schools), class distinctions in society at large would soon wither away and disappear. In fact, it was society itself which was divided in this way, and the schools have simply mirrored what society expected of them. As we have already seen, there was a tremendous gulf between the elementary schools set up after 1870, intended to give the workers that minimum amount of instruction necessary for their humble calling in life, and the traditional grammar and public schools intended to provide secondary education for their social superiors. In the nineteenth century it was essentially secondary education for some, and the some were well-defined in terms of class. You will remember that the Schools Inquiry Commission of 1868 was able to recognize three grades. The first grade provided education up to the age of 18 or 19 for the sons of rich men and professional men, who, to quote the Commission's Report 'have nothing to look to but education to keep their sons on a high social level'. The second grade was for children up to the age of 16, who entered the army or the professions; and the third grade was for a lower class—the smaller tenant farmer, the small tradesman, and the superior artisan—who wanted their children to join the family business at 14. But remember that the hymn—'The rich man in his castle, the poor man at his gate, God made them great and lowly and ordered their estate'—was accepted as a fair and proper statement at that time. It was still possible to pray, 'God bless the squire and his relations and keep us in our proper stations', and mean it. As the Fleming Report on Public Schools stated, these schools 'were in fact called into being to meet the demands of a society already deeply divided'. They may have done a great deal since to perpetuate class distinctions but they did not create them, and their perpetuation of the

107

existing order owed a great deal to the desire of society itself to avoid change. As late as 1908, Sir Robert Morant could explain in a Report to the Board of Education that the words 'secondary' and 'middle class' had been thought of as meaning the same thing, and that, 'the idea that elementary and secondary schools represent not successive stages of education but alternative kinds of education meant for different social classes is deeply rooted and may be said to have dominated practice until recently'.

But 'recently' is now sixty years ago. Though it would be idle to pretend that everything had changed in this time, and that our schools had no trace of class consciousness left in them, it is equally silly to talk as though nothing had happened, and nothing had changed. The first years of the twentieth century after the 1902 Act saw a remarkable increase in secondary schools, as the society of the time insisted that the boundaries should be thrown wider, and the 'some' deemed suitable for secondary education should become very many 'more'. After two world wars and the remarkable social changes they brought in their wake, society once again insisted that the boundaries should be thrown wider still, and the 1944 Act insisted that the schools be changed to provide a vastly enriched form of secondary education—this time 'for all'. The point I am making is that at each important stage in this development, a society with improved ideas and higher ideals insisted that it needed better schools to support and consolidate its desired progress. It was not the schools which took society by the scruff of the neck and forced it to improve itself. It was the other way round. It is arrant nonsense to suppose that the new comprehensive schools can be used by themselves as some kind of spear-head, and that in some mystic way they will rapidly change the class structure of this country. Society will have to do this for itself by using all kinds of powerful weapons, amongst which its schools is only one comparatively weak device. Unless it does this, however, the community of a comprehensive school will never achieve the complete classless integration which is supposed to be the distinguishing point between it and our existing secondary schools, and will contain in it the flaws of the world around it. To be genuinely and completely successful, a comprehensive school must be in the middle of a comprehensive community—and that is a sobering thought.

How class conscious, then, are our present, imperfect, soon
to be outmoded secondary schools? Much less so than they once
were, or than they are given credit for, and only prevented from
making further progress in this direction by the failure of society
to keep up with them. There is far too much generalization on
this point, so I will limit myself to speaking about the two
grammar schools I know best. I do not recognize either of them
in the conventional picture of a stodgy, hide-bound, tradition-
ridden institution dedicated to maintaining the interests of the
conservative middle classes, which seems to be the generally
accepted view of grammar schools in some quarters. Let us take
the origin of the pupils. It has been estimated that if measured
intelligence was the only factor in winning a place at a grammar school one might expect about sixty per cent of the children in a grammar school to come from the working classes,
and about forty per cent from the classes of non-manual, middle
class employment. Both the schools I know best have in fact a
proportion of up to sixty per cent of their pupils with a working-
class background. Though by no means all grammar schools
have this complete social cross-section—it depends largely on
the catchment area which they serve—I know many schools
which have. This illustrates the measure of the change which
has already come over the formerly middle class grammar schools
in some parts of the country since the 1944 Act. Integrating
members of all social classes into one school community will be
no revolutionary change for them—since they have been doing
it successfully for years, and glorying in it. Take the origin and
attitude of the staff. Myself included, the majority were first
generation grammar-school children themselves. That is to say
they started life in very ordinary surroundings, and progressed
by public scholarships through elementary and primary schools
to local grammar schools, and then on to universities. Five
minutes in either of the Staff Common Rooms that I know best
would convince you that they are lively, argumentative, radical-
minded people, with pronounced social consciences and a
capacity for service to the community greater than they are
ever given credit for. They give freely of their time to encourage
sporting and cultural activity, and are ready to try any new
syllabus, or course, or method, provided it can be proved to
their satisfaction that it will benefit their pupils more than the

traditional devices they have been using. In one sense they do stand for the maintenance of the *status quo* in that they use all their efforts to see that their pupils aim at the highest standards of scholarship, and lay great store by gentlemanly behaviour and appearance; and this leads them into sharp conflict with the unduly permissive, 'with it', hedonism, which is so often confused these days with a progressive and tolerant attitude; so that they are fair game for being attacked as querulous, other-worldly, fuddie-duddies. But in another and even more important sense, they are key people in a most remarkable social revolution which has taken place so quietly and unobtrusively that we completely fail to realize its importance. Since the 1944 Act the Grammar Schools have been directly responsible for a remarkable increase in social mobility. It is now a commonplace for working-class boys and girls to rise 'above their station' by means of a grammar-school education, whereas it used to be a rarity. We have shot the rigid division between the working classes and the middle classes as it existed in 1908, or indeed in 1938, so full of holes, that instead of being an iron curtain it is a leaky sieve. It gives me wry amusement to listen to doctrinaire arguments in public that the grammar schools must be swept away as they are bastions of social reactionaries; and then in private to hear quite another story. If you are joining a group of schools together to form a comprehensive school, the best chance you have that it will be successful, they then say, is to be sure to include a grammar school as the centre of the group. Of course it is. But would it be if they were the citadels of black reaction they are said to be? I have expressed my profound scepticism that the new comprehensive schools can do anything much in a frontal attack on the class structure of this country; but they can do a great deal by continuing the guerrilla warfare which grammar schools have been waging with such conspicuous success. The comprehensives now must take up the fight for increased social mobility, but their advocates should remember and be grateful for the efforts made in this direction by our out-moded schools which they are replacing.

I am, of course, aware, that this 'guerrilla warfare', as I have called it, can be viewed in a totally different light. The grammar schools, it is said, are incurably middle-class institutions, heavily committed to imposing the standards and attitudes of the middle class on all children committed to their care, and showing no mercy on or understanding of standards or attitudes which are different in any way from the accepted middle-class norm. The warfare, so the thesis goes, is not directed at the rigid division between classes, but against the working-class standards and attitudes of children from working-class homes which clash heavily with the accepted ethos of the grammar schools. Children from these homes find themselves in an unhappy no-man's-land, subject to a withering crossfire of misunderstanding and resentment from school and home. This makes the existing grammar schools fundamentally useless as a means of transmitting the central culture of our society to the working-class majority, and therefore they must go. It will be clear from the previous paragraph that this is a thesis which I find it impossible to accept, since it does not accord with reality as I have found it to be during my long experience in these schools. But this does not mean that tensions of this kind do not exist. Of course they do. When you are committed to enlarging and enriching a child's experience (as any good school must be), to encouraging it to stand on its own two feet and develop a critical and discriminating attitude to the world around it, it is absolutely inevitable that the time will come when the child is conscious of the contrast between the standards of its home and its neighbourhood on one side, and of the school and civilization in general on the other. To grow a little is always to die a little, and moments such as this when a child has to decide can be painful and disconcerting. The greater the gap between the standards of school and home, the more painful and disconcerting it can be. But a gap of sorts will continue to exist whatever label we put on the school, and the best grammar schools of the recent past have been as careful to help children to cross this gap as ever the new comprehensive schools are going to be. Bad schools of both types (and I profoundly hope they will become fewer and further between) will continue to fail, but this will have more to do with the inadequate personalities involved than with the types of school, or indeed the class origin of the pupil. I do not wish to belittle the importance of this 'gap' or these 'tensions', since the successful negotiation of these pains and perils of post-adolescence is precisely what secondary education is all about. But I do question the mechanistic assumption that the 'gap' and the 'tension' is invariably greatest for the working-class child. Sometimes yes, but quite often no. At least I never cease to be amazed at the understanding and helpful attitude of many parents of indisputably working-class origin, and as a practising headmaster I know that to have an understanding parent is the greatest gift a child can have at this difficult time.

Indeed, to discuss the social stratification of this country (or of our schools) in terms of class alone is to use dangerously misleading shorthand. There are many other factors to be considered, and in a few moments I will indicate what some of them are. But bearing in mind that with every new council housing estate that is built, and they are going up by the hundred, what I have to say on the subject of class becomes more and more outdated, there is still enough meaning in the word for us to press it a little further. Now curiously enough, the strongest opposition the grammar schools have encountered in their attempt to promote greater social mobility has come, not from the desperate defenders of hereditary privilege, but from the working-class boys and girls themselves. The comprehensive schools are going to find themselves up against this difficulty as well—and it will probably be greater in their case because as area schools they will be more directly linked with their own particular district, and correspondingly more cut off from other areas. Middle-class intellectuals with strong social consciences make the elementary mistake of imagining that the working classes feel themselves members of 'the lower orders', with other classes oppressively piled above them and regarded as their superiors, and that they are all to a man fighting to 'get out from under'. Statistical evidence is then produced to show that only a minority have succeeded in doing this, and this proves that it is black reaction that has held them down. In fact a majority of the working classes have no such ambitions, and are most unhappy when attempts are made to get them to act as though they have. They are well aware that they are in a section of the population which is a group or community of its own, but far from feeling any sense of inferiority to any other group, they have a certain fierce pride. They do not regard themselves as lonely individuals with their own way to make in the world, but rather as one of a group whose members are all roughly level and likely to remain so. This group works hard against any idea of change, and imposes on its members a harsh pressure to conform. To 'forget yourself', 'to give yourself airs', to start 'talking posh', leads to the tossing of heads, and to 'who the h— does he think he is'. In return, the family, the street, the neighbourhood, provides a peculiarly gripping wholeness of life and human warmth, quite different from anything on a middle-class housing estate; and it requires great strength of character and determination to break away from it. Within certain clearly defined limits, there is great tolerance and friendliness within the group—all men are free and equal, life is constantly changing and attractive, why shouldn't you enjoy it whilst you can, you might never be as lucky again—and all this militates against setting oneself too high standards, and striving too hard to maintain them. Those who do make an extra effort—in cleanliness, thrift, or self-respect—do so rather from a deep concern not to succumb to the environment and sink lower in the social scale, than from a burning desire to go up to a higher social strata. Because within the working class itself, there are subtle shades of class distinction—the prestige of a particular house, similar to all the others except it is at the end of the row, or you have transformed it with different curtains, or got the latest television set in the front room—the hereditary aristocracy of the street or the housing estate, who have lived there longest and can afford to condescend to the more recent arrivals—the very real distinctions at the work bench or on the shop floor between the skilled man, the unskilled and the labourer. No member of the House of Lords is more jealous and mindful of his position in society than are members of the working classes of their position *vis-à-vis* their neighbours and acquaintances. 'All men are equal' is a cheerful omnibus sentiment—but without making a song and dance about it, all members of the working classes are quietly confident that they are more equal than some other members of the working class which they could name if they had to, but don't as everybody knows who they mean. It is this cosy, clearly defined niche in society which they are anxious to maintain—and even a move to a new council housing estate, though it brings many material advantages, disrupts these well-established patterns and tends to leave them feeling rootless and ill at ease. The working classes are a very exclusive group indeed, with their own inverted snobbery, which is twice as potent as the more straightforward kind. The world is divided sharply between 'us' and 'them'; and 'them' contains not only the members of Debrett and the captains of industry, but civil servants and the police, minor local government officers and, I am afraid, teachers. 'Them' require watching to see that they do you no harm, and you must always be on your guard when you come into contact with them, because 'them' (poor misguided outsiders) are just not 'us'.

I have tried to give this thumb-nail sketch of what I believe to be the reality of the situation because if I am right it faces the comprehensive school with a fundamental problem as far as its social foundation is concerned. If you think what I have said is an exaggerated caricature, it will at least do something to correct the conventional picture, which is too far biased the other way. Every working-class boy is a life member of several natural communities with deeply ingrained characteristics long before he becomes a member of the rather artificial community of the school. There is the community of his family, his street, boys and girls of his own age in the area, the local football supporters' club, to mention only a few. These have a powerful intimate influence on him long before he comes to school, and all the time he is a member of it. They will be even stronger and more powerful when all the children of one area attend the same area school—just as today they tend to be more powerful in secondary modern schools than grammar schools, because secondary modern schools draw their pupils from a smaller catchment area. No school can afford to disregard these influences on the one hand, or to declare total war on them on the other; it has to do its best to live with them, if possible to guide them, and when it is really successful to transcend and transform them. Because these influences are parochial, conservative, and stultifying, it means that hundreds and thousands of first rate children are held back from achieving their full potential, and fail to take up their proper place in the higher strata of society.

Now I have been talking so far as if the social stratification of this country depended entirely on class, but I have been guilty of serious over-simplification. Class is a concept which, following Marx, is associated in the first place with a person's relationship to the means of production—how he gets his dole, wages, salary, dividends, or honorarium. There is another element we must take into account, and that is often referred to as status; and status depends more on the consumption of goods and services—how a man spends his dole, wages, salary, etc., and consequently his general mode of living; what Max Weber called 'life style'. Although status and class exist alongside each other and tend to influence each other in a bewildering way, it is coming to be generally accepted that social order in this country is now more closely associated with status than it is with class differences. Sociologists tend to describe these status differences, or differential life styles, by the word Culture. This should not be confused with the more ordinary and restricted use of the word as having something to do with string quartets, *avant-garde* films, or abstract painting. The word in this context has a much wider meaning—it refers to the total way of life of a society, how it eats its food, wears its clothes, uses its language, and the values and aims which are dominant in its religion, philosophy, and ideology. It is clear that the culture pattern of this country would be quite different from that of a South Sea island, or a pigmy tribe in the middle of Africa. It is also clear that inside the overall culture pattern of this country, there will be many sub-cultures differing markedly from each other, though with certain underlying similarities which would differentiate them all from the pigmy tribe. Now if class, in isolation, has a tendency to be static, and has influences which as far as the working class is concerned are educationally parochial, stultifying, and conservative, status or the wider concept of the culture pattern is the exact opposite. Never in all our history has it been more dynamic and rapidly changing—these changes being both helpful to education, and at the same time presenting more difficult problems for it.

Whilst it is still possible to detect differences between what you might loosely term the middle-class culture pattern and the working-class culture pattern of this country, it is remarkable how the differences are being blurred, and how rapidly the former is assimilating the latter. The mass production of clothes, refrigerated food and supermarkets, the hire purchase of cars and furniture, make it ever more difficult to distinguish one from the other. Cheap packaged holidays on the continent, the radio and television—see the world yourself, and invite the Prime Minister into your own living-room, if he can find a place with televised Coronations, Miss Universe or the finals of the World Cup. All this is bound to be helpful in breaking down barriers and improving attitudes towards education, and should be most helpful to the comprehensive schools in bringing about social integration inside the schools in a way which a few years ago was either impossible or very difficult.

But there is a sting in the tail. There has emerged a powerful teenage sub-culture, drawn remarkably enough from all classes of society, the like of which we have not seen before. There has been a great increase in the earnings of young workers. They have doubled in twenty years—a much quicker rate of expansion than that of adults. This spending power has, in this materialistic age, gained them great prestige. They spend extravagantly on outrageous clothes, and the mass media have created and glorified their own folk heroes—pop singers, disc jockeys etc. New techniques of work in rapidly changing industry favour the youngsters, and tend to discredit the older generation of workers in their eyes, because their old skills are useless. As the distance is increased between home and work, the ties and influence of the family and the neighbours are reduced. More and more the tendency grows for younger children to copy their example. A new loyalty has grown up for those still at school to a teenage group with its own standards and a different way of life. A gulf has opened up between the generations, and it is the first task of the new comprehensives to help to see that it is closed, or at least bridged over. This is a piece of genuine social engineering which they can and must tackle. Faced with the conspicuous anti-intellectualism of their pupils, their peer group, and in the worst cases of their parents, it is going to be an uphill task. But somehow they have to integrate these sorely troubled children into their community, and convince them that they have a positive role to play in society. Because, as was said at the end of the previous chapter, 'A school is not merely a teaching shop, it must transmit values and attitudes. . . . A child brought up in such an atmosphere at all stages of his education has some hope of becoming a balanced and mature adult and of being able to live in, to contribute to, and to look critically at the society of which he forms a part.'

EQUALITY OF OPPORTUNITY

Equality of Opportunity is a fine emotional slogan which is often bandied about without any real understanding of what it means. By many unthinking people it is glibly assumed to have something to do with 'uniformity' and 'sameness' purveyed in equal and identical schools; and it is then rejected or demanded, according to whether the individual feels 'unprivileged' and thinks he has something to gain, or feels 'privileged' and thinks he has something to lose. I have said enough already to make it plain that if and when we have a complete system of comprehensive schools each one will differ in important respects from the next one, and to expect completely identical and equal schools is to bay for the moon. Indeed we ought to welcome such differences, because they will be the signs of zest and life, and the people running the school must have the freedom to introduce such variety as seems in their professional judgment to be necessary, or else they are reduced to impersonal office-boys half-heartedly implementing a pale blue-print foisted on to them by others. Again, children are not identical blobs of 'raw material' being put through the same factory processes, to emerge at the far end as finished articles. They are individuals, differing widely in their potentialities and their needs, and it is nonsense to suggest that they are best served by being treated in school with complete 'uniformity' and complete 'sameness'.

It is important to realize the fundamental paradox which lies behind the glib phrase—Equality of Opportunity—and alone gives meaning to it. It means attacking one inequality with another. It means heavily weighting the scales in favour of some children to reduce certain inequalities from which, through no fault of their own, they are suffering; and one must clearly accept the fact that when all this has been done, the achievement of one child will be markedly different from the achievement of another. At the end of the process there will still be geese and still be swans. The phrase does not mean equal opportunity to do the same thing. Indeed, we might well get rid of the emotive and misleading word 'equal' without further delay. It means the right opportunity to do different things— and we must now analyse in detail the two halves of this definition.

How, in broadly similar comprehensive schools, can we provide the opportunities for different children to do all the different things in one school which they were previously able to do in separate grammar, technical, and secondary modern schools; and more importantly (because if we cannot do this the entire exercise has been a complete waste of time) how can we ensure that in the one school there is a far richer and more varied choice of things to do than was ever possible in the separate schools; and further, how do we make certain that these choices are more in tune with the real needs and interests of the individual children, and of this rapidly changing modern world?

The first essential is curricular reform. This would be badly needed in all our schools, even if comprehensive reorganization had never been thought of; and will in my view be seen eventually to have brought more far-reaching and lasting benefits to our children than any administrative regrouping of schools on its own can possibly do. It has long been the proud boast that the curriculum of our schools has been decided by the headmaster and staff of each school; they naturally took such advice as seemed to them helpful and relevant, but the final decisions were theirs and theirs alone. We must preserve this freedom at all costs, since if it is removed, one can hardly expect the head and the staff to shoulder any real responsibility for the school supposedly committed to their charge. But of recent years, this proud boast has become more of a boast and less of a reality, for two important reasons. Firstly, the pressures on the school from outside interested parties—universities, examiners, professional bodies, employers, and parents—have become so great that the scope for manoeuvre of the individual school has been drastically reduced, and the curricula of all schools have tended to become too congested as they attempted to shoe-horn in the new without being able to jettison the old. Secondly, there was such a bedlam of advice from interested parties with axes to grind or bees in bonnets that the heads and their staffs found it difficult to decide which parts of it were really worthwhile—and there was no disinterested body which could give the influential guidance which they so badly needed and were anxious to have. The teaching of Mathematics, for instance, was a matter of grave general concern, yet it was left to groups of interested individuals, financially supported in a variety of strange ways, to formulate their 'Projects' and arrange for their publication. Clearly, there was something fundamentally wrong with the teaching of Science, yet it was left to private bodies such as the Nuffield Foundation to work out a practical approach. I do not wish to belittle any of the efforts of this kind which have been made by interested individuals and public spirited groups, but it was a scandal that we should have had to rely so heavily on this kind of approach, since without firmer central direction there is bound to be duplication of effort and waste of time.

At long last, a central body has been set up to provide this direction, control, and stimulus, which we so badly need. This is the Schools Council. Its job is to focus the best professional brains of the country on to the interrelated problems of what should be taught to various types of children, and how it can best be taught. It will stimulate careful, fundamental research into the content of curricula and methodology—not in a theoretic vacuum—but in close contact with practical problems in real schools; for the process is a two-way one. It is envisaged that local teacher centres will be set up in every area, at which the ideas and suggestions of the Schools Council can be explained to and discussed by practising teachers. Such centres are already working in some areas, and many more will soon be opening. It is the dawn of a new era of cross-fertilization and co-operation. A great deal of useless lumber will be got rid of— the painful compilation of long lists of facts for their own sake, the laborious mechanical slog of doing things in your head the hard way, when everybody knows that it can be done much quicker by machines once the principle itself has been learnt. This will provide more time to concentrate on helping to improve the thought processes, and enable us to bring all subjects at all levels into a more direct relationship with the needs of the individual pupil and the needs of the world. It will put the spotlight too on the shape and size of the traditional classrooms— now too small for the larger groups for activities which can best be handled in groups much larger than the conventional 30, and too large for the smaller groups into which the traditional 'class' will be more and more divided for teaching/study purposes. It will emphasize the grave deficiencies in teaching equipment from which all schools now suffer, and the importance of 'aides' and ancillary workers around the school to allow the skilled teacher to concentrate on his essential teaching function. It will pin-point the areas in which extra expenditure (when it becomes available) can have the most direct impact on the learning processes of children, and I am sure that local authorities will not be slow to give priority to these things. So the state schools of the future, whatever their titles may be, will have a far better chance of getting to the heart of the matter, and doing more 'different things' for their pupils than ever they have had in the past. But this, be it noted, will be only marginally because they are comprehensive schools, and really because we have got round to providing an essential piece of co-ordinating machinery, the need for which was obvious as long ago as the Clarendon and Taunton Commissions.

Critics will say that a limiting factor for a long time has been an undue concentration on narrow academic success as the one worthwhile driving force behind our curricula, and this in itself meant that curricula tended to be unsuitable for the less academic majority. But we cannot remove this driving force for the majority (not I hope and pray for them all) without replacing it by another; and to provide clear and powerful motivation for the new and more flexible curricula, we will have to make them more outward looking. That is to say that not only must the subject-matter be within the comprehension of less able children, and be presented in lively and interesting ways calculated to maintain enthusiasm, but it must also be clear to them that it is directly relevant to the life they are going to live, and the kind of job they are likely to find themselves doing. Even if some form of streaming is retained, excessively fine grading of ability groups in the earlier years must be avoided. It will be sufficient to see to it that the groupings in the final years are largely based on sensible and appropriate choices of subject or of course. All schools will have to provide a range of courses broadly related to the occupational interests for children in the fourth and fifth years, and they will need to be adequately equipped to do this. This will mean large extensions to practical rooms for handicrafts, domestic science, and commercial activities such as typing. Care will have to be taken to see that these developments are not too narrowly vocational, since industry is changing so rapidly that twenty years from now these children will be called upon to do jobs as part of processes which have not yet been invented. But a girl may see a great deal more point in concentrating on improving her spelling and punctuation when she finds how much of a handicap her deficiencies are in typing lessons; and a boy may see more relevance in mathematics and science if pains are taken to present them to him in the context of engineering. Quite early guidance will need to be given to children so that they may choose the course most appropriate to them. This means a whole battery of aptitude tests of a kind which so far are unknown in schools, and advice on careers will have to be given much earlier and in more detail. It will have to be given its place in the curriculum as a teaching subject—leading to quite frequent visits from industrial representatives to the school to add special point to the discussions which the teachers concerned will be having with the children, and ever more frequent visits by middle-school children to works, offices, and businesses. These must not be erratic affairs—large groups of children wandering through in a daze, paying little attention to what is happening, and having only the vaguest of ideas of what it has all been about—but must be carefully planned beforehand, carefully conducted, and carefully followed up afterwards. That is to say that the teacher must spend considerable time beforehand carefully explaining the process the children are going to see, and drawing up a list of things to watch out for or questions they should be trying to answer for themselves during the visit. The conventional tour of the factory will then be more meaningful and interesting, and in certain cases it should be possible to arrange for children to be 'seconded' from school for a few days to gain genuine 'work experience'. In my view, each child should be required to keep a folder or note-book in which experience gained during successive visits could be 'written up', so that the child would have a permanent record of its own personal 'local study'. My own school has been doing this sort of thing for years with marked success. This calls for the willing co-operation of employers, a change in attitude by many Trade Unions, an alteration in the Industrial Insurance Acts, a better staffing ratio in the schools—and a bus and several mini-buses at the permanent disposal of every sizeable secondary school to cut down on the time wasted in travelling.

For the brighter children, the impact of external examinations must be, and can be, reduced. It is quite wrong that success or failure in the G.C.E. 'O' Level should depend almost entirely on performance in one three-hour paper, written under conditions of extreme nervous tension at the end of a summer term. It is not beyond the wit of man to arrange that credit be given for 'course work' done during the preceding year or so, so that a child may see that by doing its everyday work conscientiously and well it is steadily building up a positive assessment which will save it from outright failure at the very least. Again, the Schools Council is encouraging a more forward looking attitude to the methodology of examining a much broader ability range —notably through what is known as Mode 3 of the C.S.E. The trend is towards giving teachers greater responsibility for the continuous assessment of their pupils, with external moderators to ensure that standards are maintained. I think it is also important that schools should establish their own internal leaving diploma for pupils unsuitable for external examinations, which would concentrate not on attainment (probably very low in most of these cases) but on indicating the variety of effort, persistence, and interest shown. This would counteract the tendency to enter obviously unsuitable candidates for external examinations, simply on the off-chance of getting them a 'piece of paper', by which the external world sets such great store.

Finally, if a school is trying hard to widen its choice of courses, and to present them in as flexible and interesting a way as possible, it must know that in the last resort, when all else has failed, it has power to get rid of the 'wreckers'. Every school contains within it a certain number of seriously maladjusted and unbalanced children, and manages by hook or by crook to assimilate the vast majority of them into the community, and to do a great deal to help them overcome their difficulties. But it occasionally encounters an individual or small group which completely fails to respond, and these can do untold harm to themselves, to the impressionable and the weak-willed of their class-mates, and to the general well-being of the school, if they are left to fester in a community which they have so obviously rejected. There must be an increase in the number of special schools for the seriously maladjusted and chronically 'difficult' children, at which they can receive the appropriate treatment for their unfortunate condition.

So much then for 'different things'. What is to be said about providing the 'right opportunity'. All parents provide their children with an opportunity of sorts for profiting from their education. Here is the opportunity of one fourteen-year-old girl, quoted in the Newsom Report, artlessly revealed in an essay entitled 'Getting Up':

At half past four every morning the alarm clock goes off. Then I know it's time to get up. I get dressed and then go down into the coldness. First of all I put on the kettle. While that is boiling I make the fire. I make my father's porridge and shout him up for work. When he's gone I get my sister up for work. When she has gone I clean up then get ready for school. After that I shout my brother up and help him to get ready for school. Then I call my mother up.

All districts provide the children living in them with an opportunity of sorts for profiting from their education. Again the Newsom Report is relevant:

There is no need to read the melodramatic novelists to notice that there are areas, often near the decaying centres of big cities, where schools have more to contend with than the school-boy's traditional reluctance. These are the districts where, as Mr. J. B. Mays puts it, 'We find many different kinds of social problems in close association: a high proportion of mental illness, high crime and delinquency rates; and above average figures for infant mortality, tuberculosis, child neglect and cruelty. Here, too, the so-called problem families tend to congregate. Life in these localities appears to be confused and disorganized. In and about the squalid streets and narrow courts, along the landings and staircases of massive blocks of tenement flats which are slowly replacing the decayed terraces, outside garish pubs and trim betting shops, in the lights of coffee bars, cafés and chip saloons, the young people gather at night to follow with almost bored casualness the easy goals of group hedonism.' What does it feel like to be responsible for a school serving such an area?

Clearly, if anything like the right opportunities for children such as these are to be provided, two things are necessary before the teachers can really be expected to show results. There has to be a much more concerted attempt made to deal with the general complex of social problems in such areas (of which education is only one), and this will be a long and expensive business. There has also got to be, as a matter of national policy, 'positive discrimination' in favour of schools in neighbourhoods where children are most severely handicapped by home conditions. This means high priority for new, functional buildings, and improved staffing ratios for these schools. It also means that as a matter of course, a team of social workers and counsellors will have to be attached to these schools, with the time and energy to supplement the work of the teachers in these important areas.

But quite apart from the different opportunities provided by the poor home in the slum or twilight area and the good home in the pleasanter surroundings—and the many permutations one can find on this pattern, such as the good home in the bad area, and the bad home in the good area—the problem is far more complex than might be supposed. Amongst any normal group of children, however homogeneous it may appear to be, there are large differences between one child and the next, and even if this group is sitting in the best possible school in the most favoured area, these differences have to be taken into account if the individuals are to achieve anything like their true potential. This is where detailed modern research to establish the pattern of a child's growth and development is of paramount importance to people in schools trying to educate it. This has been clearly recognized in infant and junior schools, and it is a little unfortunate that the rigid division between the primary and the secondary sector has tended to obscure its even greater relevance to the older children—since the pattern of a child's growth and development is one continuous, infinitely complicated natural process, continuing on its own sweet way in its own sweet time, however much or however little we chop up and divide the schools to which we send our children. This is the old 'Nature versus Nurture' controversy brought up to date. We must take careful note of the way children develop if we are to spot which educational practices are harmful so that we can replace them by more effective ones.

The general picture of a growing child is that of a number of facets of physical, intellectual, and emotional behaviour developing slowly or quickly, according to the individual and his circumstances; 'according to the individual' in the sense that every child is born with 'genes', which are the means of transmitting hereditary influences from one generation to the next. These genetic factors operate throughout the whole period of growth. Some are active at birth, some only become active at later stages—which probably accounts for the way children begin to resemble their parents more closely as they get older. 'According to his circumstances' in the sense that his environment—his mother's womb, his cradle, his home, his neighbours, his school—continues to exert powerful influences on his development at all times. Some of these environmental factors have an obvious and immediate effect from the very beginning; others have what is known as the 'sleeper' effect, and have little obvious effect when they are most obviously operative, but can come to life at a much later stage when they are not expected to do so. Taking a child's physical development as an example (because this is more easily measured), it is clear that it contains a sequence of stages—each stage fixed in definite order, but each stage starting and finishing at widely different chronological ages, according to the complex and continuous interaction between the developing organism of the child and its environment. The rate at which a child is travelling through these stages towards the physical maturity of the adult is known as its developmental age, and it can be markedly different from the child's chronological age. A common way of estimating this developmental age is by measuring the maturity of the skeleton —particularly the bones of the hand and the wrist, in which the sequence of changes can be seen by X-ray. Amongst boys of the same chronological age there is a wide range of bone age—a group of eight-year olds, for instance, may range from six to ten 'developmental' years. There is also marked difference between the sexes. At birth the average girl is already some weeks ahead in 'developmental' age of the average boy, and she gradually draws more and more ahead until at puberty the difference is two years. Girls are also more resilient than boys under adverse conditions. With the increasing move towards co-education these differences between the sexes are important. Environment can also be seen to be having an effect when we notice the difference in average body size between children of different social classes, or socio-economic groups as they are called. The difference in average height at present, for instance, between children in upper middle class homes and unskilled workers' homes is about one inch at the age of five, rising to one and a half or one and three quarter inches at adolescence. Although we know significantly less about the physical development of the brain cells and the organization of that remarkable organ, it does seem clear that certain functions are localized in particular parts of the brain, and that these again mature in regular sequence—first the motor area, then the sensory, then the visual, then the auditory—but at differing rates. So it is fairly clear that as well as physical development there is an equivalent emotional and intellectual development taking place, which may be retarded or advanced by external circumstances but is basically a natural process, taking place at its own pace, and that a different one in each child. All these facets of development may be, and probably are, at a different stage of their development, not only in different children, but in the same child. So a 12-year-old boy might be beginning puberty, might be strong and big for his age group, and outstandingly good at all games, and yet be well behind his contemporaries in formal 'school work', not because he was lazy, not because he was 'dim and would never be any good at it', but simply because he had developed more slowly in these respects and would not reach maturity in this respect for him until a later chronological age. We are in fact, asking him to run and jump and perform intellectual gymnastics before he has grown his intellectual legs, and by the time they have grown we may have destroyed his confidence in them, and his desire to use them, and made sure that he really is 'dim' and 'lazy'. 'Forgive them, for they know not what they do', is the only comment on some of our best-intentioned efforts.

The first reaction to all this is that we should be extremely sceptical of politicians and administrators who try to tell us that all there is to comprehensive reorganization is to abolish segregation by ability into different schools by sending all children to one common school, and that the ideal age for this to happen is not 11+ but 12+, 13+, 14+, or some other magical, but quite arbitrary, chronological age, which by some strange coincidence just happens to suit the buildings they have available. It is true that by abolishing segregation by ability you make greater flexibility theoretically possible, but they remain curiously blind to the fact that children in state schools are to remain firmly imprisoned in the strait-jacket of their chronological age. I shall have more to say in the next chapter on the harmful effects of this on our brightest children. Meanwhile, it is sufficient to point out that if we were to arrange children according to their height, weight and strength (i.e. their physical development age), it would be as useful, and as misleading, as relying entirely on chronological age. The real comprehensive reorganization will come when we stop juggling with the administrative patterns of schools, and get down to fundamental research on the intellectual, emotional, and physical development of children of all ages; provide schools with diagnostic tests so that they can periodically check the point of development at which each individual child has arrived in all three; and advise teachers and parents of the appropriate treatment required. Then it will be possible to get much nearer providing the 'right opportunity' for every child.

But whilst we are waiting for all this, we can at least use intelligently the knowledge we already possess; and this indicates very clearly that if one genuinely wants to equalize opportunity one starts, not in the middle of the educational process, but right at the very beginning.

Spoken language (says the Plowden Report), plays a central role in learning. Parents in talking to their children help them to find words to express, as much to themselves as to others, their needs, feelings and experiences. Through language children can transform their active, questing response to the environment into a more precise form, and learn to manipulate it more economically and effectively. The complex perceptual-motor skills of reading and writing are based in their first stages upon speech, and the wealth and variety of experience from which effective language develops. Language originates as a means of expressing feeling, establishing contact with others and bringing about desired responses from them; these remain fundamental functions of language, even at a more mature level. Language develops through the stages of speech, to repeating the commands and prohibitions of others, to become finally part of the child's internal equipment for thinking.

Now a child's active vocabulary grows, or should grow, at a dramatic rate between two and five years, reaching an average of over 2,000 words. It has been estimated that a child needs to understand about 3,000 words before it is ready to start reading. A child coming from a home where the forms of speech are restricted is at a serious disadvantage before it ever enters an infant school. It has not had the chance to acquire the necessary vocabulary, and to be placed in a new social situation without adequate powers of communication can be quite traumatic. This blocks it from full participation with the rest of the infant group, delays it in reaching the point when it can start to learn to read, and may even adversely affect its development in school for the rest of its career. By and large, the majority of children adversely affected in this way—left at the post before the race has even started—come from the poorer working-class homes— the very section of the community whom comprehensive re-organization is intended to help most.

It is not good enough to wait until they have drifted through to the secondary stage, and then try to provide them with the 'right opportunity'. By then it is far too late. They need the verbal stimulus, the opportunities for constructive play, a more richly differentiated environment, and the access to medical care that at least part-time attendance at a good nursery school could provide. The object should be, not to replace the home, but to supplement it. Yet the under fives are the only age group for whom no extra educational provision of any kind has been made since 1944. We have raised the school leaving age at the other end, abolished all age schools, expanded university and further education, and done a little bit for the youth service. Clearly, a large expansion of nursery schools should have a high priority.

Nor should the primary schools—that essential link—be for-gotten. Quite simply, the provision of sufficient teachers to reduce the size of primary classes to 30 is the one reform of all others calculated to have the most powerful effect in real terms. The best of these schools are superb already, and collectively they are doing a fine job—but one would like to see them all given the chance to really 'go to town' which the reduction in the size of classes would give. Then, and only then, would we have a firm foundation on which the reorganized secondary schools could build to provide all their pupils with what for them would be the 'right opportunity'.

I imagine that, as usual, the teachers in the less fortunate secondary schools will be left to struggle against impossible odds, with only the minimum of support from authorities, both central and local, in the building of this essential structure. There will be much polite talk of the economic difficulties of the country, which will disguise the lack of a proper sense of urgency and priorities for education amongst the electorate at large. It is most important therefore that comprehensive schools in the future should be able to, in fact should go out of their way to, make more direct and fruitful contact with the parents in their area. By this I do not mean just the establishment of Parent Teacher Associations—useful bodies on the whole, but curiously patchy and unsatisfactory organizations when you rely too heavily on them—but rather that schools should strive as a matter of policy to use any increase in facilities which may come their way, to establish a relationship between themselves and their area similar to that of the famous Cambridgeshire Village Colleges. I have seen a new purpose-built comprehensive which has got itself a double-sized swimming pool, sports hall, theatre and library, by the simple process of arranging to share these facilities with adult organizations in the evening. This seems to work well in this case. It enables this school in a good area to act as a magnet, drawing adult interest and enthusiasm to it, and getting valuable appreciation and understanding of the difficult task it is engaged in. It enables the school in a poor area to act as a beacon, lighting up, however flickeringly and uncertainly, the intellectual and spiritual darkness which surrounds it, and helping in some small way to reduce the cultural poverty of the area. Parental attitudes of parents towards the school may then start to change, to the mutual benefit of all concerned. Certainly the school should try to tap the strengths and remedy the weaknesses of its immediate area.

Nor should it forget the importance of the aesthetic subjects to the general emotional development of every child. Art, crafts heavy and light, and music should have their place in the scheme of things for a whole variety of reasons, not least because they have for too long been regarded by some people as matters which can be left out of a child's education without any harm being done—or even as the province of the child less bright at other school work. They are, in fact, a part of every child's birthright—and one of the bright spots of recent years has been the way this has come to be generally recognized. One would hope that there would be an expansion of the time and facilities made available for them, since it is the school's job to help its children towards a sense of proper aesthetic values, and to lay the foundations of good taste.

This is all part of the general pastoral care that a good school takes of its pupils, and this has never been more necessary than it is now. There is an immense potentiality for good in the young, yet there are aspects of our present society which threaten its full development. I do not say that society is worse than it once was, because for a great many youngsters it is a good deal better than in previous ages. But it is certainly different, and there are so many factors in it that are neutral, that is to say capable of both good and evil. The flood of scientific knowledge, for instance, has blessed us with a whole armoury of gadgets—motor scooters, transistor radios, the pill, the T.V.—which we do not fully understand and cannot really control. It has also weakened the impact of religion, which has ceased for the majority (temporarily I would hope) to be the unquestionable basis for moral behaviour. From one point of view it is good that adults have lost their overwhelming certainty that they know the difference between right and wrong, because this has stopped the tendency to dictate moral standards to the young and expect them to accept them unthinkingly—which they never did. From another point of view it is bad, since it has so undermined the confidence of the adults in these matters that their relationship with the young now shows an unduly permissive, even apologetic attitude. Again increased affluence, the necessity to purchase status symbols with it, advertising media driving one to do so, and hire-purchase making it possible to get it today and pay for it later—has a powerful effect on the greedy acquisitiveness and the exhibitionistic instincts of all ages. Yet this is not an argument for returning to a state of abject poverty. Nor would anyone seriously suggest that we should get back to the state we were in before the Welfare State cushioned us against the worst economic pressures of sickness and unemployment, but our newly-won security has made us less inclined to fend for ourselves when in difficulties. The increasing mobility of the population, and the large size of

factories, trade-unions, housing estates, football crowds etc.,
where personality is submerged and lost in an amorphous mass,
and the break-down of close-knit families which all this tends
to promote, presents the youngster with a baffling maze, and he
needs to be provided with certain clear guide-lines to help him
find his way through it. It is up to the adult world to find a way
through the gap which now exists between the generations to provide these guide-lines; and the schools must play a leading part.

They should try to provide security, not just in material
things ('He's got everything money can buy, and we can't do a
thing with him.') but in the setting of high standards of kindly
justice and consideration for others. The school community
needs to 'demand as well as to provide, to deny as well as to give;
to denounce as well as to condone; to act as an electric charge
as well as a feather-bed; to be guaranteed and inexhaustible, but
to command respect and perhaps even a little awe'. The time
is past when religious beliefs could be imposed, but this does
not exonerate the school from helping its pupil to consider
carefully the difficulties of reconciling established religion with
the modern world, and providing him with a few ideas which
much later may crystallize into a personal faith of his own—
since the spiritual development of any human being is stunted
until he has faced up to the mystery of his own appearance
in, and departure from, this world. For in the last resort, 'it is
not buildings, programmes, organizations which build up our
young people for their future, but other human beings able to
speak to their condition and in contemporary terms, yet still
conveying, with humour and humility but courage and con-
viction, the basic truths to which men constantly return.'

The final test as to whether our schools have succeeded in
providing the right opportunity for their pupils to do different
things is to be seen in their improved behaviour and greater
confidence in conducting their difficult personal relationships
in a rapidly changing world. This is what is meant by 'Equality
of Opportunity'.

MAINTAINING INTELLECTUAL STANDARDS

And what of the third matter of general concern—that there is
a pool of untapped ability amongst our children—a good deal

of wasted talent which the tripartite system has so far been unable to utilize—will the new comprehensives be able to do anything about this? It is to be hoped so, as there will be bitter disappointment all round if they fail. But it would not be wise to assume that it will follow automatically. We are part way towards it by ensuring that children of all abilities are in one common school, and that it can provide many different courses for children whose need is different—but we are only part way. There is a certain danger that by operating on such a broad front we may dissipate our energies, and the impact of the school be correspondingly reduced. Again, our emphasis on the social function of the school, and the complex administrative machine necessary to make anything like a reality of this, may divert further attention from what is the fundamental purpose of any school, and that is, to be a machine for teaching—a place where children can get knowledge and practice skills.

You may remember the reasons given in the Clarendon Report of 1864 for the retention of Classics as the principal study in the traditional endowed grammar schools of those days.

For the instruction of boys it is material that there should be some one principal branch of study, invested with a recognized and, if possible, a traditional importance, to which the principal weight should be assigned. . . . We believe that this is necessary in order to concentrate attention, to stimulate industry, to supply to the whole school a common ground of literary interest, and a common path of promotion. . . .

I quote once more this curiously old-fashioned remark, partly to show how far we have travelled towards a child-centred school since those days; and partly to emphasize that there is now no one single subject which could unite a whole secondary school today as Classics was once fondly supposed to do. But more importantly still, I want to stress how 'material' it is for every school to have some point of unity to which the 'principal weight' can be assigned in order to 'concentrate attention' and to 'stimulate industry'. Since this rallying point can no longer be a subject, it must be an attitude, a frame of mind.

If our schools are to maintain their drive and purpose, and not to become flabby boneless wonders, they must at this point come into direct and painful conflict with the spirit of the age, and with some of the less happy ideas of educational reformers. They must latch on to the old-fashioned schoolmasterly attitude that the important task of every day is to bring about a personal confrontation between teacher and pupil, at the end of which a lesson has been well and truly learnt, and that there is positive virtue in insisting on hard work and high standards. This is a frame of mind which is conscious of the limitations of a particular child, but not too conscious, and goes out of its way to extend a pupil to his fullest extent, sacrificing some personal popularity on the way, but drawing from his pupil a long-term respect, which is far more valuable. If our schools are to be less narrowly 'academic' in future, they must establish a background and atmosphere which is as deeply and genuinely 'intellectual' as ever it has been in the past; and the replanning of curricula must be done on this basis.

Far too often, I am afraid, it may not be, largely because people are confused about the three essential stages in planning any curriculum—objectives, content, and method. 'Objectives' are the development you expect to bring about in children over a period of time—the qualities of mind, attitudes, values, and skills, as well as the knowledge you hope they will have gained. Clearly, the 'content', the matter you propose to teach over this period, should be chosen in such a way that it helps towards achieving these objectives; and the 'method', the way in which you set about teaching the matter, should be chosen with the strengths and weaknesses of the group of children in mind, and can and should vary widely when teaching the same matter to different individuals and groups. Objectives, content, and method, are of course closely connected with each other, but this is all the more reason why we should keep them carefully separate in our minds if we are to advance into the future with confidence.

Although the better schools have made great efforts to get as far away from this weakness as possible, I think it is still fair to say that the traditional curriculum of the conventional grammar school is powerfully affected by the limited range of its objectives. I would not wish to gainsay for a moment their emphasis on the all-round development of the individual—games, school plays, orchestras, foreign visits, and all the rest of it. But at the heart of the matter is their insistence on the mastery of certain areas of well-established knowledge, the learning of a number of skills, and the development of qualities of mind directly associated with academic learning; and this is their central objective. The 'content' used to achieve this objective is largely, though by no means entirely, a corpus of principles and facts which have to be learnt, together with material for practising certain relevant skills, divided fairly rigidly into 'subjects' which tend to exist in isolation from each other in watertight compartments. Their 'methods' are still (though they are now changing quite rapidly) largely the formal procedures of the class-room, relying heavily on the traditional mixture of chalk and talk. The success or otherwise of their efforts is judged by a system of external examinations designed to test just these limited academic objectives that I have been outlining.

Now before the attack starts on this bald caricature of what a conventional grammar school is, let me hasten to add that these limited objectives, which I have so far described as a weakness, are also the grammar schools' greatest strength. They were clearly understood by staff, pupils, and parents alike, and it was possible for all concerned to concentrate their energies on achieving them. This gave everyone connected with these schools a strong sense of purpose, a clear sense of the direction in which they ought to be heading. The very fact of their high local prestige—that parents strained every nerve to get their children into them—showed how much this success was appreciated. This was their point of unity, the heart of their tradition —the attitude, the frame of mind to which I was just now referring.

The new comprehensive schools are being launched with very much wider objectives, attempting to influence human and social developments in a far more pretentious way over a much greater field. The danger is that their objectives will be too wide, too all inclusive, too imprecise for them to be really effective, and a good deal of what they purport to be doing may remain little more than a pious platitude, hoped for but never achieved. As their objectives are broadened, so the content of their curricula becomes much less rigidly predetermined, and is visualized more in terms of topics or practical projects designed to be of interest to children, rather than in terms of logically developing subjects. There is a tendency to further imprecision—to the playing down of the importance of the mastery of prescribed areas of study, in favour of a superficial acquaintance with much broader fields. There is much greater stress on informal methods, direct practical experience, and activity for its own sake. Indeed, in extreme cases, the curriculum seems to be little more than an elaborate device to fill in the time available as pleasantly and painlessly as possible, where the gimmicky, eye-catching publicity stunt takes precedence over the hum-drum slog of the prosaic educational essentials. Do not mis-understand me. I am not saying that wider objectives, more varied content, and livelier methods are wrong, but that one can go too far, too quickly, along this road, and lose all intel-lectual discipline in the process.

Although children vary in their capacities and abilities, if they are to get from their school anything that will be of per-manent value to them, they need this intellectual discipline. There is an unfortunate anti-intellectualism abroad today preaching a more comfortable code of concentrating on 'interest' and the 'practical'—and to my mind this can lead to dull mediocrity and unachieved potential. It is far too readily assumed that linguistic and abstract forms of thought are not suitable for the majority of people, and that they must be allowed to retreat as quickly as possible into arts, crafts, and practical activities of all kinds, as these are thought to be more suitable for the less intellectually able. Now these pursuits have an important part to play in the development of all children—the ablest as well as the least able. But it is still necessary for the less able child, at the appropriate level, to concentrate on the development of his linguistic skills however rudimentary, and to wrestle with abstract ideas however simplified they may have to be, so that he too may have learnt to think in his own fashion and at his own level as well as his more able contemporary.

You have cheated him of his birthright if you have prevented him achieving this amount of self-fulfilment, however limited it may be; and he will remain a vegetable rather than a rational human being however hard you protest to the contrary. This is in no sense an attack on the appropriate use of livelier methods, and more interesting and practical approaches to the problems of learning; simply an insistence on the paramount importance of the 'content' of the syllabus. Apply as much sugar to the

135

pill or gilt to the gingerbread as you like—but the central core must be there or else all the trimmings are in vain.

What this central 'content' should be in the changed conditions of the new comprehensive schools is far too large a question to answer completely at this point, but here are a few suggestions of some of the lines it might well take. Almost certainly, I think, there will be greater emphasis on the practical subjects than has been possible in the past. These I would define as the Newsom Report does, as those occasions in the school day when children spend their time away from classrooms and desks—art, crafts of all kinds, music, physical education, wood and metalwork, rural studies, housecraft and needlework. These will be added to as time goes on, when it becomes possible to introduce as a matter of course things like photography, film making, improvised drama, and social service, all of which already have their place in the liveliest schools. Practical subjects will become more important for two reasons. One is in their own right. They give an opportunity for the exercise of skills other than the purely academic. Many of the average or less than average children—though by no means all —can find through these practical subjects a sense of achievement which has so far escaped them in more strictly scholastic activities. Ill at ease with abstractions and ideas, many will welcome the opportunity of grappling with what at first sight seems to them to be a more limited problem in a more practical situation. It is easier for them to see the link between this school activity and the real world of men and women outside school, and it has more relevance to their future activities either at work or in the home. But as they roll up their sleeves and don their overalls or their aprons they find themselves faced by a real challenge. This activity is also demanding in its own special way. The piece of wood, the strip of metal, the dress length of material, impose their own discipline on the craftsman or craftswoman, which is subtly different to the teacher-imposed discipline of other subjects; and unless they react properly to this discipline of the material and handle the situation in the right way, they will ruin the stool, the wall bracket, or the two-piece outfit, and they will have deprived themselves of the pride and pleasure of a definite and measurable achievement. They feel themselves under great pressure to avoid this at all costs, and are very receptive of the hints, and advice, and instructions of the teacher which can help to improve their own deficient skills. They are asking to be taught, not having meaningless lessons imposed on them, and it is this state of mind which can not only maintain their interest in the practical lessons themselves, but also spill over to the rest of the curriculum and energize the rest of their work in other subjects. For the second reason for giving greater importance to practical subjects is the powerful 'fifth column' effect they can have in arousing interest in the more scholastic subjects of the curriculum, and proving to the children that they too are 'practical' in their own way, providing of course that these subjects have taken the trouble to meet the children half way in this respect. A teacher of practical subjects must therefore seize all his chances, not just the chance to teach special skills in his own subject, if the time given to him is to be fully justified. He must realize that the unusually close and confidential relationship with his pupils which his subject encourages enables him to reinforce the importance of their understanding of the use of language and number, and to develop their powers of reasoning and judgement: the fundamental importance of being able to give and receive, orally or in writing, clear and concise instructions, or else you finish up with an object that nobody wanted; the importance, again, of accurate measurement and careful computation, or else you run out of cloth, or finish with one leg of the stool shorter than the others. Why is it better to do the job in this way, rather than another? Is there, in fact, a better way of doing it than the one which has been tried? Each of these practical experiences, if it is to justify fully the time spent on it, should lead to thought and expression, and not be regarded as a substitute for thought and expression for the less intelligent. The teacher must be sensitive to appreciate when he can push out the narrow confines of his own subject to include fields normally regarded as the province of other subjects, and to bring to the pupil's attention the relevance of the small object he has just created to wider aspects of human experience. Any craft can lead to the consideration of other things made by man—houses, furniture, clothes, jewellery, interior decorations. How have these been affected by different climates and social customs—which is Geography. How have they been managed in the past as opposed to the present—which is History. Any consideration of man-made designs or colour schemes can lead on to the consideration of how such things are handled in the natural world—which is Botany, Zoology, and might even at times lead in the general direction of Theology. A teacher who brings out connections such as these will start his pupils thinking, give them ideas, and at the same time provide them with a vocabulary in which to express them. Wall displays and diagrammatic illustrations, books of pictures and explanatory articles will help to break down the old-fashioned idea that these are 'non-bookish' subjects for 'non-bookish' pupils. The practical subjects should set themselves out to provide a rewarding discipline of the hand, the eye, but above all of the intellect.

There must be a similar readiness in other parts of the curriculum to step over the rigid subject lines, and reinforce and support one another, and to cultivate a more practical and realistic approach. For instance, wherever the pupil looks in the world around him, in school and out, is 'science', and what we teach as science in school should aim to gain immediacy by relating itself whenever possible to everyday examples and illustrations. It is, indeed, a 'practical' subject in its own right, as the advances in what can be called 'Nuffield Science' show. The aim is to provide each child with an inexpensive piece of apparatus with which he can 'do' an experiment, and from this activity and experience a train of thought is started and is followed. To get full value, a good deal of careful and unhurried discussion is needed, so that the pupil can decide exactly what it is that has been discovered about the physical laws of the world around him from his exercise. The fatal mistake is to try to cram in too much, to disappear too quickly up too many productive alleys, since if you try to fill up extra time with additional subject-matter, you cut down on the essential 'digestion' period, and quantity has seriously affected the quality. Quite apart from its own intrinsic value of giving some idea of a scientific approach to the mysteries of the physical world, have you noticed how admirably suited the time marked out on the time-table for the teaching of science is for using and strengthening the other basic skills usually considered as having more to do with English and Mathematics? Because to discuss what the experiment seems to have proved is a fine exercise in the use of words, and a painless method of increasing a boy's vocabulary, and helping him towards expressing himself more fluently. Then again, there is an opportunity for practice in reading, by occasionally using written work sheets or general guidance cards to give the pupil written instructions which he must decipher, or by directing him to books of reference in which he can check the universal relevance, or irrelevance, of his own private theory, which he has just proved to his own satisfaction by experimentation. It is, of course, essential that once a discovery has been made, discussed, and authenticated that it should be recorded in writing for future reference; and good written records of this kind can give shape and precision to what would otherwise be a chancy and untidy process of learning. They help to give the pupil confidence from the sense that something has been successfully accomplished, and there is the notebook, and diagram, and simple calculation, to prove it. They also give continuity and coherence to the course, and as the cumulative record builds up the intellectual framework of general scientific ideas which we hope the pupil will discover for himself gradually becomes apparent. It is not only apparent, but it means something to him, because he has had a hand at all stages in its emergence. His own Law means more to him than Boyle's Law ever would have done, even though they both may say very much the same sort of thing. But unless this distillation of experience and thought takes place—at either a low level or a high level according to the ability of the pupil— the subject has utterly failed to provide a proper intellectual discipline for the child, and has been about as pointless to him as doing a jig-saw puzzle from which the important pieces are missing.

There is, of course, a ferment in the field of Mathematics, and the whole flavour and range of this subject in Primary Schools is changing out of all recognition. There is no doubt that the Secondary Schools of the future will be able to base their teaching of mathematics on foundations of interest and understanding greater than ever they have been in the past. But this should not blind us to the inescapable fact that the essential tools for success in any practical mathematics is still a sound knowledge of elementary arithmetic—addition, subtraction, multiplication, and division—and these essential tools will require to be used and sharpened throughout the secondary school. A mere endless repetition of elementary exercises in the secondary school will not put this right. The reintroduction of calculation as a necessary part of some more adult and practical task that the pupils are anxious to do well but which cannot be tackled without some arithmetic can be enormously helpful. The maths lesson cannot afford to exist in a vacuum of disembodied figures, but must attract to itself the human interests of the world around it—cricket averages, soccer transfer fees, personal budgeting, darts scores, rates of pay. There are a thousand and one possibilities. There is much that the sensible teacher can do to arouse fresh interest, and to reduce unnecessary drudgery, whilst still persisting with the same basic skills. What he cannot do is to pretend either to himself or the child that calculating machines and computers have removed all necessity for the school to provide some competence in elementary calculation, and some understanding of mathematical ideas for its pupils. He must tackle the irreducible task which still remains, since without some competence in this field the processes of thought in other activities and other subjects are hopelessly stunted.

Indeed, the principal lesson is the interdependence of all subjects, and since teachers have been so slow to spot this we need hardly be surprised that it has tended to be less than obvious to their pupils. They must, in fact, grow closer together in the future than they have been in the past, and this is nowhere more essential than in that group of subjects that we can loosely term the Humanities—things like English, Languages, History and Geography. English is, and always must remain a subject which is primarily concerned with the use and care of words. It is now tending to outgrow its former heavy emphasis on the importance of the written word rather than the spoken word, though there will always be a need for careful practice in various forms of written composition. It is being more and more realized that the overriding aim of English teaching should be to help (along with other subjects) in the personal development and growing social competence of the pupils, and that speech has a tremendously important contribution to make towards such development. If a boy can be encouraged to speak easily, clearly, and with interest then he is immeasurably strengthened as a

human being, and interesting experiments with improvised
drama and other devices are now being used to achieve this,
though Caldwell Cook was blazing the same trail at the Perse
School with his Play Way before the First World War. There is
an increasingly oral approach to the study of modern languages
too, which is making it possible for children from a much wider
ability range than in the past to take up their study with profit.
It is now possible to record a child's steady development in
oral work at various stages in its progress through the school, and
this gives a great incentive towards greater efforts, both in his
own language and a foreign language. It also adds backbone
and point to this oral work, and enables the teacher to evaluate
the success or otherwise of his own work. Now English is
especially noteworthy since its main stock-in-trade—the use of
language—provides the essential medium for every other subject in the curriculum; and furthermore by its very nature is
constantly importing to its lessons subject-matter which properly
belong to other disciplines. Why not? Here it seems to me is an
important unifying influence—a 'point of unity' as the Clarendon Report would have called it—an opportunity for team
teaching, projects, integrated schemes of work, and all manner
of useful co-operation between colleagues. Before a boy can
pluck up courage to say something—whether orally or on
paper—he needs something to say, an idea that he feels is
sensible and worth saying. Does it matter if he has picked up
the idea in a lesson labelled History or Geography? Does it
matter if he is encouraged to express it in lessons other than
those labelled English? I think not. It is of course important
that the syllabus of both History and Geography should retain
their own intellectual coherence, since they are valuable disciplines in their own right, but this does not mean that they cannot profit by coming into a closer co-operation with themselves
and other subjects. And of course they already are doing this,
and this tendency will increase. Greater integration of subjects,
an increased awareness of what each can provide for the child on
its own and in co-operation with other disciplines, is, I am sure,
going to cut out a great deal of uncoordinated, duplicated,
and often wasted effort, and provide a good deal more elbow-
room within the school day by means of which, if it is properly
used, it may well be possible for intellectual standards to be

maintained, and to be spread over a wider area of ability than has so far been possible.

But I repeat that the new comprehensive schools, if they are to be successful in this, must take over and increase tendencies which already exist in our more forward looking schools, grammar and secondary modern alike, and must take over and maintain one old-fashioned virtue which has been the main tenet of all grammar schools as long as they have been in existence. That is to say that the highest priority must be given to insisting that each child should aim at the highest intellectual standards (the highest, that is, that the particular child is capable of attaining, and almost certainly much higher than the child thought it was capable of achieving). Then there seems little doubt that the new schools will be able to make use of a great deal of the wasted talent about which people are so justifiably concerned. This will go a long way towards maintaining acceptable intellectual standards over a wider area of ability than has been so far possible, but will it also solve the problem of maintaining and improving the educational opportunities of the brilliant child? Contrary to popular belief they are by no means well catered for now. Will not the needs of this small but important minority be overlooked in the large, multi-purpose, state comprehensive schools? In theory no, but in practice it might well happen, and we must consider this danger in some detail.

The fundamental difficulty is that in our increasingly egalitarian society, the age of the common man, it is more and more difficult to persuade people that the brilliant child exists, or that if he does he merits special treatment. It savours too much of giving an unfair advantage to someone who has already been given more natural ability than the rest of us, and can only result in setting him still further ahead of us and apart from us, in some cosy and exclusive elite. This they are not prepared to tolerate. As De Tocqueville puts it,

The nearer the citizens are drawn to the common level of an equal and similar condition, the less prone does each man become to place implicit faith in a certain man or a certain class of men.... Democratic institutions awaken and foster a passion for equality which they can never entirely satisfy. This complete equality eludes the grasp of the people at the very moment at which it thinks to hold it fast. . . . Whatever transcends their own limits appears to be an obstacle to their desires, and there is no kind of superiority, however legitimate it may be, which is not irksome in their sight.

But irksome or not, it is the brain-power and leadership of these uncommon children, in the form of scientific inventions, industrial progress, and social improvements, on which millions of common men in these islands depend. This country just cannot afford to be bled to death by a double brain-drain—the much-publicized one which happens when under-valued academics at the end of their university course set sail for America —the less noticed one when a brilliant child is allowed to fritter away his potential and get nowhere, because the appropriate stimulus and treatment is not available when it is most needed. Nearly nine hundred years ago, Wang Anshih wrote his famous essay, 'Deploring Chung Yun'. At the age of five, Chung Yun had written poems which surprised the local scholars and made him quite a celebrity, but no one thought to send him to school. Wang met him when he was twelve, and found he was still writing poems, but they were not as good now as might have been expected. Seven years later, Wang went again to his village, and found to his astonishment that Chung had grown into a very ordinary man indeed. His bitter comment was,

Chung Yun's talent was given by Nature. What he has received from Nature far exceeded that received by common man. But in the end he became a common man. A person so gifted as is Chung Yun nevertheless became a common man for the very reason that he lacked help from man. Those who are neither gifted by Nature nor helped by man could not even become common people.

We should spend far more time than we do deploring our own Chung Yuns, and doing something about them.

Perhaps the sensible thing to do is to accept that outstanding intellectual gifts are not so much advantages to the person concerned as handicaps and afflictions from which he has to suffer. They certainly set him far apart from the more normal person, and make it difficult for him to settle down to the cosy, jog-trot mediocrity which satisfies the majority of us. Nobody objects to additional money being spent on a blind person, or a deaf person, or a juvenile delinquent to allow him the kind of special education he needs to allow him to play his full part in society. We must be prepared to do the same for the brilliant child, to help him overcome his disability—particularly since the return he can make to society in later life is of such outstanding importance.

Early diagnosis is both essential and possible. Whatever doubts there may be about the efficacy of intelligence testing across the entire range of ability, there is no doubt that the kind of child I am thinking of stands out very clearly in such tests—which put him in the top 2 or 3 per cent of the population on basic intelligence alone, and show him to be a good many years ahead of his chronological age as far as mental development is concerned. Much oftener than is realized, he is also ahead in physical and emotional development, and if this is the case it is particularly unfortunate to confine him to a group of children of his own chronological age, with whom he has nothing in common. He finds the work childish, and either develops habits of lazy, dawdling, dreary inattention to what is going on around him, whilst escaping into a world of his own private fantasies; or becomes a dominant, domineering exhibitionist, constantly displaying his own superiority, and earning in return the dislike and disapproval of the rest of the children in his group. When his mental age runs far ahead of either his emotional or his physical development, or both, his situation is even more complex and difficult, and to the untrained observer he may easily give the impression of being very retarded rather than the reverse.

It is worth quoting an actual case to show what I mean. Here is one mentioned by Mary Waddington in her essay on 'Problems of Educating Gifted Young Children', though similar instances could be provided by any experienced infant and junior teacher from her own experience.

Robin was not quite five years old when his mother brought him to school and asked that he should not go into the reception class as he could not only read, but was a member of the public library, and would be deeply hurt if he were put in 'the Babies'. The head mistress happened to have her copy of 'The Listener' on her desk. From this Robin read with expression: 'In the late eighteenth century, Louis XVIth . . . ' The head mistress asked: 'Robin, what do you mean by the eighteenth century?'

'Oh, in the seventeen hundreds somewhere.'

'What do es the late eighteenth century mean?'

'Perhaps abo ut 1789, or about that time, don't you think?'

This, I think you will agree is a pretty abnormal response to get from a child before its first day in the infant school. It shows a remarkable grasp of abstract ideas, and an ability to handle them in language. But suppose Robin had not been fortunate enough to be born in a family which understood these things, and where he could get access to books and ideas? How many children of similar ability are unfortunate in this way, and fail to develop to anything like their full capacity? Robin was put straight into a class of seven-year olds, but not with the happiest of results.

His teacher found him 'un-natural', and hoped for him to spit, or hit, or throw a temper tantrum, but he continued to kick pebbles on the edge of the playground, always alone. Each week his mother came to school, saying: 'Please may Robin do harder work? He is bored. He hates school.' Finally, 'Last night I heard him say to his sister that he is not going to try any more; school is a silly, sissy place, with nothing interesting.' The head mistress and the mother decided to call in the county psychologist, and the child proved to have a mental age of twelve years. Up till then Robin in school had been an expressionless little 'pudding face', but when he came from the psychologist's test his eyes were bright and his face animated. For the first time his intellect had been stretched. To cut a long story short, this child was given individual teaching at grammar school level in the infant school, with one session each week at the clinic for special teaching, and he began to mix with other children, picking the highly intelligent of all ages with unerring skill as his close friends, and being on friendly terms with the rest.

Now the story of Robin has a happy ending, but from it a disquieting moral can be drawn.

When he was seven, the local education authority sent him as a boarder to a preparatory school, where he entered a class of nine-year olds, and is now happy and successful, working three years ahead of his chronological age in one of our most academic public schools. Without a persistent mother and an understanding head mistress he would be dragging his way, bored and isolated, through the junior school.

Full marks, too, to the realistic local authority which solved the problem of getting this boy individual attention in small classes working at an intellectual pace much nearer to his own—but how disquieting that the boy had to leave the state schools at the tender age of seven, and enter the private sector, before this could be achieved.

Here is a gap which should be filled. I happen to know something of the professional skill which exists in the state infant and junior schools, and the extraordinary lengths to which teachers will go to provide such brilliant children with the opportunities which they need. They have chalked up a surprising number of successes in this field. They could do far more with smaller classes and greater flexibility—and in the overall moves to improve facilities for the average child, special provision should be made in future for this important minority. These provisions, it seems to me, must continue through into the secondary stage, and whether the problem can be solved within a multi-purpose comprehensive school, or will require to be tackled in a separate institution, is a matter on which there is hot debate.

Exactly what is required? There must, of course, be wide opportunities for their non-academic interests such as arts, crafts, and music, which they may well pursue to extraordinary standards; but mainly they must be given the opportunity to use fully their unusual ability in handling words or mathematical symbols, in playing with ideas and abstractions. Here an acute conflict can arise between giving them a broad general education or allowing them to specialize on the fields in which they are most interested, and when this does arise it is probably wisest to allow them really to get their teeth into their own specialization. Frustrating this urge can be most dangerous, and their study in depth will draw to their attention so many related subjects that they will in due course achieve surprising breadth as well. As they are so willing to learn, are they easy to teach? Is it merely a case of doling out masses of information to docile minds? With such burning interest, cannot one just put them in a library and leave them to teach themselves? There is an element of truth in this, but it is a dangerous over-simplification. More than other children they need the constant stimulus and personal attention of a body of teachers who are themselves of a really high intellectual standard. As Lord James has said, special qualities are required by the teacher of the brilliant child. His task is not only that of selecting the most effective presentation and showing the other attributes of good teaching method—the purely technical problems of pedagogy—it is also the mastering of material of considerable intrinsic difficulty. Particularly, if he is concerned with the senior forms, he must maintain a high standard of scholarship; he must constantly expand his knowledge and keep abreast of new developments, not only in his own subject but ideally in other fields of thought. . . . It is so often pointed out that a brilliant scholar may not be a good teacher (though, in fact, he is much more likely to be even that than is a third-rate one), that we are in danger of forgetting that, if a high academic standard is not a sufficient qualification, it is at any rate an absolutely necessary one for the teacher of the brilliant child. There are few more stimulating experiences for a teacher than to recognize among his pupils a mind that is obviously in a higher class than his own, but if the gap is too wide, and if the teacher simply does not understand the work that his pupils are doing, whatever his gifts as a 'teacher', his usefulness will not be very great. Thus, faced with the prospect of educating minds as intelligent as those which we are discussing, the teacher should show certain qualities in addition to pure teaching ability if he is to make his full contribution. His knowledge must be great enough for him not only to be able to teach to a very high standard, but to admit ignorance. He must be prepared to show understanding and tolerance for the extreme opinions that will often be thrown out by the turbulence of rapid growth.

Such teachers are far rarer than is generally supposed.

With comprehensive reorganization they are likely to be spread more thinly over a much greater number of schools—and in many cases will find work in Colleges of Education and Universities more attractive to them than teaching in schools. There will be a similar dispersion of the brilliant children, leading in too many cases to their isolation from the competition of equally able contemporaries; and in this isolation they may well develop a greater sense of superiority over their school mates and a weaker sense of respect for them than if they had been segregated from them in a completely separate school. A partial solution would be to provide an individual pupil of this kind with a specially accelerated course, but this removes him from the environment of his contemporaries, and marks him out once more as something unusual. Another would be to give him a specially enriched course, but this would be difficult to arrange unless the school had a most generous staffing ratio, and even then it would not be a real substitute for solid teaching appropriate to that child's ability. These drawbacks would be greatest on the child with poor economic and social background in a comprehensive school serving a poor area—and I should have thought it was precisely these children from whom one could expect to find really significant numbers whose ability in the past had been wasted.

Is this an argument for the retention of all Grammar Schools? I think not, since most of them in their present state are not really suited to cope with these children anyway. If they must be changed, they are probably of more use to society in providing the intellectual basis and standards of good area schools for children of more widely varied ability. But it is a case for providing, firmly within the state system of comprehensive schools, regional facilities for dealing properly with these special children, and really outstanding local authority grammar schools such as the one I am privileged to serve might well have been ear-marked for this purpose.

Let me take it, as an example, to show what I mean. It starts with certain advantages for this work that money cannot buy, or administrative fiat create—tradition, staff, know-how, and long experience of successful work up to university level— but it would have to change remarkably to provide the full opportunities for its future pupils that I think they need. Instead of taking in each year 150 reasonably bright children, it would take in far fewer (possibly 30 to 40 at the most) of really brilliant children drawn from a much wider area, and from all social classes. Though it would remain predominantly and principally a day school, to ensure that its pupils remained socially integrated with the area and their families, it would need to have boarding houses—partly to cater for children from a distance, partly to help children from the poorest of homes, partly to ensure that all the children at some time had experience of living together, and partly for an even more important reason which I will mention in a moment. It would need to have an out-patients' department to help infants and junior schools presented with the problem of 'Robin'. Advice and materials could be provided so that the work Robin was doing there could be 'enriched', and arrangements made for him to come into the senior school on a particular afternoon to have the stimulus of working with more adult equipment. As soon as Robin—or Janet—was sufficiently mature emotionally and physically—they would leave their junior school, and be allowed to start on their secondary studies, without having to wait for any particular chronological age. This would not be a case of 'forcing them on', but simply of seeing that they were not senselessly and arbitrarily held back. Because of all this, the curriculum would need to be extremely flexible, though at all times challengingly intellectual, and the teaching would take the form of tutorial work with small groups rather than class teaching as we now know it. The efforts of the staff would be augmented by that of visiting consultants, from the neighbouring College of Education and the near-by University. From the one would come the latest of educational techniques, and an opportunity for lecturers and students to try their hand at this most demanding work. From the other would come direct contact with the expanding horizons of knowledge, and the great stimulus to these unusual children of meeting people engaged in a wide variety of research. Just imagine the searching questions they would ask, and the gleam there would be in their eyes as they saw the stupendous nature of the problems not yet solved, and which they themselves might one day solve.

But would not all this mean isolating them from the rest of the world in their own ivory tower? It needn't mean anything of the kind. There is no reason why the closest of connections could not be maintained with neighbouring comprehensive schools of a more orthodox nature, with exchanges and secondment of staff and pupils and joint activities at appropriate times. A closed circuit television link between the schools might also help. Again, it would be most important to allow freedom of transfer from other schools to this 'special' school at the sixth form level, of boys and girls of much more modest ability, though still capable of 'A' Level work. It seems to me there would be great mutual gain from this at this stage of their development, and it would destroy any feeling of 'exclusiveness' if it was known that the gates were wide open at the appropriate time for those who particularly wanted to get in. Nor need this sap the strength of the sixth forms of the other schools—since the 'special' school could cater for unusual subjects or courses which it would be uneconomic for all schools to provide.

And finally, I would visualize a complete revolution in the teaching of modern languages to these brilliant children. This is why the boarding houses I mentioned before would be particularly useful. A great deal of time could be saved in the earlier years by reducing the time spent on formal language instruction during normal lesson periods. This would be made up for by sending these children in appropriate groups to live and work in a foreign school for two months of each year, and arranging for a comparable group of foreign children from that country to spend a similar time living and working in an English school. A working knowledge of the commoner European languages would, as these children grew older, pave the way to similar visits beyond the iron curtain, as some knowledge of Russian and Oriental Languages would seem to be most desirable for them. The problems this would cause would be great, but the rewards would be priceless in wider horizons and better international understanding. I would hope that the great industrial and commercial firms in the City would make scholarships available so that equivalently gifted coloured children from backward countries could join this school community as normal pupils—with obvious advantages to themselves and our own boys and girls. What I have in mind is more of a 'united nations', a 'junior university', than what we have so far known in this country as a school. It is absurdly parochial when dealing with children of this calibre to limit their experience to the narrow confines of the area school in which they are living. They are citizens of the world, and should be given the chance to get to know it at first hand as soon as possible.

It is important to tap the large pool of lower ability amongst more normal children, just as it is to encourage the barely perceptible ability amongst the really backward; but we must let neither of these worthy things prevent us from providing first rate facilities within the state system for the outstandingly able. I am really asking for something which is neither further education nor secondary education, but an infinitely flexible 'tertiary school' somewhere in between and beyond both these well-known concepts. 'Tertiary Schools' will have to come some day, though I confess that that day has seldom seemed so far away as it does just at present. The tragedy is that when we do get around to realizing that we need them, we will find that the rare and unusual grammar schools ideally suited to being 'Tertiary Schools' will have long since been converted into something else.

That something else will be of great value too, provided it has not been brought about by a surgical break with the better traditions of the school's past, which may unfortunately have happened in far too many areas. As I sit at my desk and the terms flick past, one of the great joys of life is the steady stream of Old Boys who come back to see the old place. It is fascinating to share their anecdotage, and to see the place through their eyes and not my own. Obviously they have to refocus a little, as buildings one knew in one's youth to be large and imposing tend mysteriously to shrink in size when revisited in later life; but once they have made the necessary allowances they almost invariably say the same thing. How little it has altered. Here are the same form rooms, the same laboratories, the same holly hedge, the same trees; and by the time I have heard the inside story of how they gave old so-and-so the run around in their day, I make a mental note that human nature hasn't changed much either.

But as we chat a little further another point rapidly emerges. When they get below the surface and hear of new subjects, developing curricula, expanded out of school activities of a cultural and sporting kind, the constant reshaping and experimentation which invariably goes on in a lively school, they all say the same thing. How much of it has changed! Rip Van Winkle, you remember, came back after snoozing away a lifetime in the ten-pin bowling rink up in the sky to be faced by the same disturbing paradox. Nothing had altered in his native village, yet everything and everybody had changed. Though outwardly this school is the same it always was, it is in fact a very different place to what it was ten, twenty, or thirty years ago. Now as the hedges and some of the trees come down to accommodate new comprehensive extensions, the rate of change is obviously accelerating.

But if much changes, much I hope will still remain. What, for Rip Van Winkle, was nothing but a disturbing paradox, is for me something much more valuable. For a school to be able to change itself with the utmost flexibility to meet the demands of a rapidly changing society, and at the same time to remain true and unaltered in the eyes of the previous generations who have passed through it, is to have established a live and active tradition. I am optimistic enough to believe that traditions of this kind are strong enough to survive the present changes, and will be invaluable in the new pattern of schools that is just starting to emerge. I find myself therefore in good heart and spirits, my head honourably bloody, but completely and unrepentantly unbowed.

Index

Index

Forster, W. E., 10, 16, 17; *see* Education Acts
Foundation Period, 93, 96
French Revolution, 10

G.C.E., 30, 44, 47, 55, 57, 59, 60, 71, 78, 84, 93, 97, 100, 122
Gloucester, 12
Great Exhibition (1851), 23

Hadow Report (1926), 31, 32, 42, 43, 95, 96, 101
Half our Future, see Newsom Report
Hazlitt, W., 49, 50
Headmasters' Conference, 17
Head Teachers' Association, 72
Holmes, Sherlock, 24
House System, 90–1
Humanities, 140

Industrial Insurance Act, 121
Inspectors, H.M., 14, 16
Intelligence Quotient, 46, 95
Isle of Wight, 47

James, Lord, 146
Johnson, Dr. S, 18
Joint Four, 72
Junior Technical Schools, 30–1
Juvenile Delinquency, 38
Juvenile Employment Bureaux, 28

Kay-Shuttleworth, Sir J, 12
King's College School, 19

Leeds Grammar School, 18
Leicestershire, 47, 55
Lincoln, Bishop of, 7
Liverpool College, 19
Lloyd George, D., 26
Local Government Act (1888), 23
Locke, J., 9, 10, 11
London, 47, 55, 57
London, City of, School, 19
Lowe, R., 14, 15

Manchester, Bishop of, 27, 29

Manchester Grammar School, 23
Manchester Ship Canal, 17
Marlborough, 19
Marx, K., 114
Mays, J. B., 123
McMillan, M., 28
Mechanics Institutes, 11
Merchant Guilds, 8
Milton, J., 9
Monastic Schools, 7, 10
Monitorial System, 12
Morant, Sir R., 108
Morning Assembly, 92
Multilateral Schools, 58–9

Napoleon, 10
N.A.S., 72
National Foundation for Educational Research, 43
National Society, 12
'Nature versus Nurture', 124
Newcastle Commission, 13, 27
Newsom Report, 39, 40, 41, 50, 99, 123, 136
Normanton Grammar School, 19
Northumberland, 43
Norwood, Sir C., 8
Nuffield Foundation, 119, 138
Nursery Schools, 34, 38, 65, 128
N.U.T., 18, 72

Owen, R., 10–1

Parent Teacher Associations, 129
Paris Exhibition (1867), 23
'Parity of Esteem', 38
Part III Authorities, 27, 33
'Payment by Results', 14
Peel, Sir R., 11
Perse School, 141
Play Way, 141
Plowden Report, 65, 102, 104, 127
Pope Adrian IV, 7
Privy Council, 13, 14
Proprietary Schools, 19
Provision of Meals Act (1906), 28